CREATING A PROPHETIC LIFESTYLE

BECOME THE SEER

FATHER MEANT YOU TO BE

Yinka Oyekan

Copyright © 2018 Yinka Oyekan.
All rights reserved.

ISBN: 9781791777593

All Rights Reserved © Yinka Oyekan. This book is sold subject to the condition that it shall not, by way of trade or otherwise, be lent, re-sold, hired out or otherwise circulated without the author's prior consent in any form of binding or cover other than that in which it is published.

It is also illegal to photocopy, scan and store electronically or otherwise reproduce any portion of this publication without the written consent of the author.

Bible Copyright

Bible scripture quotations used in this work are from the following. Bibles:

Scripture quotations marked (ESV) are from The Holy Bible English Standard Version Copyright © 2016 by Crossway Bibles a division of Good news Publishers. Used by permission. All rights reserved

Scripture quotations marked (GNT) are taken from the Good News Translation Bible © 1994 published by the Bible Societies/HarperCollins Publishers Ltd UK, Good News Bible© American Bible Society 1966, 1971, 1976, 1992. Used with permission.'

Scripture quotations marked (NRSV) are taken from The New Revised Standard Version of the Bible, copyright © 1989 Division of Christian Education of the National Council of the Churches of Christ in the United States of America. and are used by permission. All rights reserved.

Scripture quotations marked (NKJV) are taken from
The New King James Version®. Copyright © 1982 by Thomas Nelson. Used by permission. All rights reserved.

Scripture quotations marked (RSV) are taken from The Revised Standard Version of the Bible, copyright © 1946, 1952, and 1971 the Division of Christian Education of the National Council of the Churches of Christ in the United States of America. Used by permission. All rights reserved.

Scripture quotations marked (NIV) are taken from The Holy Bible, New International Version®, NIV®. Copyright © 1973, 1978, 1984, 2011 by Biblica, Inc.™ Used by permission of Zondervan. All rights reserved worldwide. www.zondervan.com The "NIV" and "New International Version" are trademarks registered in the United States Patent and Trademark Office by Biblica, Inc.™

Scripture quotations marked (LEB) are from the Lexham English Bible. Copyright 2012 Logos Bible Software. Lexham is a registered trademark of Logos Bible Software.

Scripture quotations marked (DARBY) are from the 1890 Darby Bible (Public Domain)

Scripture quotations marked (KJV) are from the *Holy Bible: King James Version.* electronic ed. of the 1769 edition of the 1611 Authorized Version. Bellingham WA: Logos Research Systems, Inc., 1995. Print.

DEDICATION

Thank you to my wonderful wife Fiona for all her support

CONTENTS

THE PROPHETIC WIND	7
PROPHECY IS A WINDOW OF INSPIRATION	26
PROPHETIC ACCURACY PRODUCES CONFIDENCE	48
PROPHECY ALIGNS OUR WILL WITH HEAVEN	58
UNDERSTANDING PROPHECY	79
THE HABITATION OF A PROPHET	92
THE PROPHETIC POWER OF AGREEMENT	99
HOW TO INTERPRET AND ACTIVATE PROPHETIC ANALOGIES	111
ESCHATOLOGICAL HOPE, THE MANNA OF RENEWAL	123
PROPHECY CHALLENGES VALUES AND MINISTRY	139
MAKE THE MOST OF EVERY OPPORTUNITY	150
THE FATHER'S VOICE	162

"The last days will see a revival of prophecy, the likes of which the world has never seen before, as God's sons and daughters prophesy without fear or restraint."

The Prophetic Wind

When the wind of God begins to blow over a network of churches, a church, or a person, it heralds the start of a beautiful adventure. It means the divine will is about to become incarnated in that individual or body of people, at the expense of natural laws, if necessary, and almost certainly in the face of opposition.

"Prophecy is the paintbrush behind the picture called 'a fruitful life'."

Once the prophetic is activated, excitement builds, as does a sense of awe. In the current of the prophetic, new life, energy and hope are birthed. This book is intended to help encourage the activation of the prophetic, to bring the voice of heaven down to earth, and to help groups understand the strategic significance of prophecy in both their life and the lives of their loved ones.

THE BREATH OF GOD

The Prophetic is the "Ruach" or Breath of God

Ruach is the Hebrew word for breath. The action of speaking is only possible because of the exhalation of air, and so it is said we, or in this case God, "breathes" or "speaks". Resulting in two key effects.

Genesis 1:3 And God said, "Let there be light," and there was light. NIV

The first consequence of God speaking is the release of creative and constructive or sometimes destructive energy.[1] His spoken words sweep the heavens and the earth, bring forth life in the form of vegetation and blessing, but release the floods and plagues when there is corrective intent. Herein are both the ecstasy and the pain of this gift rolled into one. The prophetic aroma of heaven which the believer embodies, is to resistant hearts the smell of death.[2] Moses was such a fragrance in Egypt. To the citizens of Egypt and the Hebraic slaves, Moses was a great deliverer, the aroma of freedom; but to the Egyptians, he was the herald of doom, the bringer of plagues and trouble of their peace. Why? Because Moses had received a prophetic message from God which would set the destiny of both his life and the nation.

Thus, when someone receives a prophetic word, that person is being invited by God to look through a window in time, to share in the knowledge of an imminent creative act of God, destined to transform the lives of those who hear forever.

"Prophecy is the shining of a brilliant light on the road called destiny."

The second consequence of God speaking is illumination, the shedding of light, for every word from God is bathed in the brilliance

---

[1] Prophecy releases creative spiritual energy seen in; The creation of the heavens and earth; healings emotional, physical and spiritual; vision as received by Moses, John the Baptist and Solomon in his desire to build the temple. Prophecy always produces something.

[2] 2 Cor 2:15-16

and the glory of his presence. It illuminates people's lives giving in some cases a photographic snapshot, in others just a glimpse; sometimes this picture is extraordinarily detailed.

I was praying recently In Croydon for a group of people who had long-term sicknesses and diseases, and several of them were healed. The trigger for the healings was three prophetic words for specific individuals in the congregation. As I listened to God, he eventually led me to take a stand against long-term sicknesses and diseases.

After the meeting as I was preparing to leave, one of the ladies who had been healed was seen dancing around the hall, she danced over to us then danced up the platform steps inviting us to bear witness to the fact that she had been healed from long-term chronic arthritis, explaining in particular, the significance of her ability to walk up the stairs pain free after many years of suffering.

At the moment of prayer for these precious souls, I can say with confidence that I heard the Holy Spirit tell me that he was going to heal. I can with joy recall how over the years the Holy Spirit has spoken to me in some amazing ways just when I needed to hear him the most.

The lady In Croydon who was healed of the long-term sickness reveals another aspect to the power of prophecy.

The prophetic wind of the Spirit moves obstacles out of the way; the breath of God uproots them. This is how God dealt with the Red Sea when it presented itself as an obstacle to God's redemption of Israel from Egypt.[3] For the onlookers stuck between the Egyptian army and the Red Sea, the question they would have asked themselves would have been "where do we go from here?" But God turned what looked like a dead end into a highway of hope, literally through a troubled sea.

The Prophetic Realm is Alien to Flesh

The seeming otherworldliness of prophecy is a result of a lack of intimacy with God. God predicts, because time has no closed doors or windows to him. God has the ability to see the whole picture and the unlimited capacity to work miracles in order to achieve his objectives. This can make the experience of prophecy quite strange, because time is essentially a closed book to every other type of being, without exception. Even if we did know the future, we do not have the power to make much of a dent on it, because we lack the ability to control it. Many people for instance, have theoretical knowledge of how to make money on the stock exchange, but few can actually turn that knowledge into any real profit, those who can are paid extraordinary amounts of money because it is an extraordinary skill. Even then there is no guarantee that there will be profit.

The language of prophecy enhances this sense of otherworldliness because prophecy is full of mysterious language requiring interpretation and encrypted symbols requiring decoding. The carnal mind is easily troubled and can be confused by it. This is particularly true when God is speaking to a group or individuals who have a poor "spiritual" relationship with him. Conversely, for those who are

---

[3] *Exodus 14:19-21 "Then the angel of God, who had been travelling in front of Israel's army, withdrew and went behind them. The pillar of cloud also moved from in front and stood behind them, 20 coming between the armies of Egypt and Israel. Throughout the night the cloud brought darkness to the one side and light to the other side; so neither went near the other all night long".*

"spirit-filled" and pursue intimacy with God, choosing to live in his presence, the prophetic realm is not so discomforting, but it can still be hard to understand.

When God commands us to speak prophetically or sends a prophetic message, it is a message of hope, warning or challenge, but it always signals his intention to transform the circumstances.[4] For the prophet finds that seeking to impart God's will, or communicating, can be fraught with difficulties of presentation, least of which is the perception that the prophet is odd.[5] While this is sometimes true of Old Testament prophets, the good news is it does not have to be true of New Testament prophets. We are not proponents of the weird, but chaperones into the presence of God.

The desire to know the future is an inherent part of the human condition which Satan uses, seeking to draw people into alternative spirituality.[6] Those with a prophetic gifting help people find their way. Only God truly has the power to make the future his business, and he stamps his authority on it. The scriptures say he "knows the end from the beginning". For the recipient of the prophetic voice, the challenge to respond in faith[7] to God's display of his knowledge of the

---

[4] *Ezekiel 37:1-14*

[5] *Every Prophet stands out in their generation, their message being primarily for the people living in their day and their message containing moral and spiritual challenges. The way they dress or dramatise the prophetic message can also cause them to stand out.*

[6] *See "The Supernatural World, Yinka Oyekan chapter 1*

[7] <u>*The response of faith*</u>

- *How does one acquire faith? – faith comes by hearing the word of God Rom 10:17*
- *How does faith increase? – faith increases through hearing God speak into the human heart*
- *What faith is not - faith is not a muscle, it is not an emotion, it does not originate with man but with God, as Christ is the initiator and finisher of faith.*

future, is a challenge to trust him, a challenge that leaves the recipient with only two choices; accept and obey or reject and disobey. The ultimate question of prophecy is, do you trust God with your life?[8]

"Prophesying is to prophecy what rehearsals are to a concert."

If spiritual understanding is to liberate and naturalise the mind of the believer to this other world, a reprogramming of the mind and heart needs to take place. If the carnal mindset[9] is to be broken and reprogrammed to allow us to become comfortable with insights into our spiritual destiny and publicly profess received prophetic revelation, both the rehearsal and regurgitation of prophecy privately are important.

This basic personal groundwork of the soul and mind is not only a preparation for that day of opportunity when the prophecy becomes a reality and opportunity to be grasped, entered into and taken, it also helps us to articulate to others what we understand of the

---

- *Prayer James 1:2-7; Works James 5:13-14*
- *Has a measure Rom 12:3*

[8] *Hebrews 11:6 and "without faith it is impossible to please God, because anyone who comes to him must believe that he exists and that he rewards those who earnestly seek him."*

[9] <u>The Carnal Mindset</u>

- *The sinful mind is hostile to God Rom 8:5-8*
- *The sinful nature and the indwelling Spirit are in conflict (Gal 5:17).*
- *Has its thoughts set on things that lead to death as opposed to the mind of the spirit which is life*
- *The sinful mind does not submit to God's laws nor can it do so.*
- *Puffs up Col 2:18*

prophecy becoming embedded in our hearts, enhancing our supernatural disposition.[10]

The Significance of Rattling Bones

In the example of Ezekiel 37, God asks the prophet if the dry bones could live. [11] Within the context of normal human experience, we know the answer to the question is no. But in the context of divine inquisition, the prophet answers rightly *"you alone know"*. What a question and what a response.

> *"Past fulfilment is the current foundation for prophecy."*

God uses his fulfilment of past prophecy and the display of miracles, as a foundation for new prophecy. In Ezekiel 37, the prophet continued to prophesy as God began to perform the miracle, pulling bone to bone and commanding flesh and muscle to appear. The sound of the rattling bones in the Ezekiel 37 passage is the sound of God beginning to fulfil the miracle. This symbolic moment of the rattling of the bones is the most significant moment for the

---

[10] *The Supernatural Disposition*

Lives by faith 2 Cor 5:6-7; Gal 3:10-14; Sings col 3:16; Feeds 1 Pet 2:2; is being built with others 1 Pet 2:5;attains wisdom Col 1:9;Fights battles Eph 6:12;heals and restores others Gal 6:1; Imparts; offers sacrifices; Rom 12:1; has spiritual gifts 1 Cor 12:1

[11] *Ezekiel 37:1-5 "The hand of the LORD was upon me, and he brought me out by the Spirit of the LORD and set me in the middle of a valley; it was full of bones. 2 He led me back and forth among them, and I saw a great many bones on the floor of the valley, bones that were very dry. 3 He asked me, "Son of man, can these bones live?" I said, "O Sovereign LORD, you alone know." 4 Then he said to me, "Prophesy to these bones and say to them, `Dry bones, hear the word of the LORD! 5 This is what the Sovereign LORD says to these bones: I will make breath enter you, and you will come to life. "*

beneficiaries of the prophetic voice, for it is in this moment that all is lost or won in the heart of the recipient. The point at which the individual embraces the fusion of the fourth and fifth dimensions,[12] choosing to live in the reality of that which has not yet come to pass, as though it has.

The Prophetic Wind can be an Electrifying Sound

Several years ago, Fiona and I took a party to Hungary on a mission trip. It was quite exciting with many saved and the local pastor encouraged. One meeting we attended was extraordinary. We had started the meeting with a drama which was an interesting exercise, as it had to be translated into Hungarian as the actors said their lines, a hilarious experience. Then as I began to preach the word, some latecomers arrived. They were gypsies. One of them, a lady, had started to seek spirituality and had previously bought some books on witchcraft, which she had begun to read. She had decided to come along to the meeting because the previous night as she slept, someone appeared to her in her dreams and said that tomorrow people would be coming to the town.

She was told in the dream that she had to go and hear what they had to say. I knew none of this of course and simply preached a gospel message to which she responded. She then proceeded to tell me her story through an interpreter. I was of course worried as to the meaning of the dream; I was particularly worried as to whether she would look elsewhere for help. When I quizzed her a bit more, she said through her interpreter "well the person I saw in my dream was standing next to you as you spoke, so I knew I was in the right place, but he has disappeared". When she said this, we were all astonished,

---

[12] *time and the spiritual world*

the air felt as if it was charged with electricity and we knew God was with us, all of us were right in the centre of God's will and plan, and we knew that he had brought us to this small town.

This was the second time (to my knowledge) that the Lord had given dreams to complete strangers telling them I was visiting their town. The first time this had happened was in Ghana where a king and his entire family gave their lives to the Lord, because the king had been warned six years earlier that I would be coming to visit him.

Walking with God in the Whirlwind of the Spirit

"The eye of the storm is where all the good weather is in a hurricane of trouble."

The prophetic wind offers a chance to walk with God in the adventure of a lifetime, which will feel at times like a rollercoaster ride. A unique opportunity is presented through the prophetic unlike any other, to journey in the eye of the storm.

It is often understood that the safest place to be when the hurricane comes, is right at the centre of the eye of the storm. And so, when God decides that he is going to speak into a particular context, the hearer's greatest challenge will be to "keep in step with the spirit", meaning to be obedient regardless of the personal difficulties faced.

> *2 Samuel 22:11 "He mounted the cherubim and flew; he soared on the wings of the wind". NIV*

The prophetic wind coming to prominence within the life of the church denotes that God is on the move. Invariably the prophetic move will undoubtedly bring a clash with national and personal agendas. This is not aggression on his part, because fundamentally

God is love and so his motivation for the prophetic will always be to demonstrate his love and avert his anger to bring people into loving relationship and a better life. If his anger were ever the cause of this move, it would result in a storm that no one would be able to withstand and, in whose path, no one would wish to be found. Understanding that love is what motivates God's dealings with us does not remove the dramatic turbulence which follows the prophetic voice, nor does it mitigate the sense of unease that can accompany it.

I remember the very first prophetic word that God gave me for an elder of our church when I was a young Christian, as I shared it with him it was astonishing. He was a high flying and respected worker in the financial industry in Scotland. I sat down with him as a young lad and delivered a very specific word concerning his personal walk. I could tell he was a bit apprehensive before I began, as the church I attended at the time was not charismatic and so the idea of God giving prophetic words was a bit suspect. Nevertheless, this elder was willing to suffer a young lad patiently. It was fascinating as this man who usually looked entirely composed and extraordinarily well groomed, melted in his chair as the prophetic opened up his worldview, and in humility, he accepted that what I brought to him was very much a word from God.

Of course, I respected him more for it, not least because this was not a charismatic church. I had started by explaining to him that I was not sure that what I had received was right. He humbly confirmed that I was right and that I should pray for him.

Many years ago, I experienced this same initial sense of apprehension when on the first day of my first ever visit to the big apple, a stranger came up to me in a park and started prophesying over me saying "you will plant many churches and write many books". At the time it was confirmation of what I believed the Lord to be saying to me and was what Fiona and I had been doing. Indeed, from the moment God spoke we resolved not to let that word go, but to hold onto it until we had obeyed it and to this day, we still live in the benefit and hope of it.

The scripture in 2 Thessalonians outlines an incredible but open secret; Satan will be unseated by a word[13] (breath) from the mouth of the returning Christ and thrown down (destroyed) by his glory. It is pride in rebellion to God which blows Satan and all rebels away, like specks of dust in a tornado.

The result of God speaking could be that stars are flung into space; his voice can command seas to part, or nations to crumble. The sensitivity and delivery of a prophetic creative act could be so gentle that one could miss it if one were not keenly listening.

> *1 Kings 19:11-12 The LORD said, "Go out and stand on the mountain in the presence of the LORD, for the LORD is about to pass by." Then a great and powerful wind tore the mountains apart and shattered the rocks before the LORD, but the LORD was not in the wind. After the wind there was an earthquake, but the LORD was not in the earthquake. 12 After the earthquake came a fire, but the LORD was not in the fire. And after the fire came a gentle whisper. NIV*

This sequence of events would undoubtedly have caused Elijah to pay attention. I can imagine Elijah ducking for cover at the sound of shattering rocks. I can imagine him grabbing hold of the ledge he was standing on for dear life. I can imagine him feeling less than secure as

---

[13] 2 Thessalonians 2:8 "And then the lawless one will be revealed, whom the Lord Jesus will overthrow with the breath of his mouth and destroy by the splendour of his coming". NIV

the wind picked up the pace and as an earthquake shook the earth beneath his feet.

The way God speaks to him is indeed most illuminating, Elijah a humble prophet was spoken to in a humble voice. God speaks to him in a whisper. A mode of speech which necessitates drawing closer to the speaker, leaning in to hear what is being gently whispered, requiring the listener to listen a little more intently.

The difference between God's whispers and man's, is that God's whispers can crack open mountains, and when it comes to people, his whispers can melt hearts.

I fear that many believers who do not impact their environment and transform the world, will fail to do so, not because of a lack of prophetic revelation, but rather because many of us are living hectic lifestyles, meaning fewer of us are taking the time to stop and listen. How many times did God speak to Israel? How often did they listen to what he had to say? And even when they heard clearly, how often did they do the opposite of what he was asking them to do?

The spiritually aware believer then embraces the creative breath of God and by so doing is illuminated. If he presses in and makes it past the seeming otherworldliness of prophecy, he will begin to decipher its language. Discerning the first signs of prophetic fulfilment, the believer will not be discouraged by the turbulence in the wake of God speaking.

THE HEARTBEAT OF PROPHECY

"The prophetic life is like a musical instrument tuned by God, in harmony with heaven."

Churches are Desperate for Relevance

Most churches are desperate to make some kind of impact on the communities which surround them. The danger they face in seeking to accomplish this is to only pick up on short-term and fashionable trends. To see if, somehow, they can apply a teaching, acquire a skill set, or some knowledge that would help them either make the church more relevant, or perhaps at least popular.

Many years ago, the Holy Spirit began to move the church I was then leading, into what can best be described as a twofold prophetic stream. On the one hand, God was calling us to leadership in the town, which seemed a strange notion because we were not a big church. On the other hand, he was calling us very clearly to grow the church through groups. Not being entirely clear what kind of groups. This was to come much later.

We embarked upon the latter with zeal, experiencing a measure of success as people came to faith in Christ. Ordinary individuals became extraordinary. The gentlest members became the greatest soul winners. One of them a young Zimbabwean lady began to introduce many of her cousins and a broader network of friends to Christ. At one point there were over forty of them building a community, with at least twelve of her family and friends saved.

This process only came to an end when one of their family members, thought by all to be a pastor, turned up. His inconsistent lifestyle gave excuse and reason for several of the new converts to lose their way. I am sure that many churches and communities may have similar stories to tell of a strong, imposing, or even charismatic character leading folk astray. The lesson of the breakthrough was not lost on me, the impact of seeing several seemingly ordinary church members displaying astonishing ability was firmly embedded in my consciousness.

"The Testimony of Jesus is the heartbeat of prophecy."

What had made the difference with this particular group of individuals was the way a simple but an honest expression of love to Christ was communicated. Their lives prophesied Christ. Now scripture informs us that the testimony of Jesus is the spirit of prophecy. Without this unashamed proclamation, or testifying to Christ, relevance to the world will be limited. Therefore, when a prophetic wind blows, evangelism naturally follows. I have no doubt that at the point a church receives and moves towards, or experiences, a fresh prophetic wind beneath its sails; evangelism becomes one of the natural outcomes. In the case of the church I was leading above, I found myself suddenly surrounded by a community full of people who seemed to be drawing in non-Christians, with minimal effort; everything seemed effortless. Recently in the church I now lead, something similar happened after three years of being drawn into renewal.

"The fuel behind evangelism is prophecy."

Right at the core of every prophetic wind, is the inherent desire to testify to Christ's accomplished victory, the spirit of testimony which is the lifeblood that flows right at the heart of Christian prophetic utterance.

> *Revelation 19:10 At this I fell at his feet to worship him. But he said to me, "Do not do it! I am a fellow servant with you and with your brothers who hold to the testimony of Jesus. Worship God! <u>For the testimony of Jesus is the spirit of prophecy.</u>"*

The fuel behind evangelism is prophecy which is the open secret, the doorway through which churches can become relevant. With hearing and obeying, whether personally, corporately or socially, comes an evangelistic release, that is not contrived or forced, connecting us through the "voice of God" to the world. In obeying, we discover that there is no more magnificent evangelistic program than hearing from heaven.

Prophecy's Effect on the Church

Prophecy is so important that it is listed as the second-ranked gift that God appoints[14] in the church. Because of its nature, i.e. the spirit of testimony, it features in every answered prayer, and every scriptural promise testified to in any church community. Once testimonies of God's goodness are released, they become an irrepressible part of a community lifestyle. If there is a lack of prophecy in a church and such a church decides to encourage testimony actively, then prophetic incidents will exponentially increase in the life of that church.

"Like a warm smile prophecy is infectious. Drawing in the human soul."

Picture the scene in the early church; the believers are praying for Peter who is in jail, when suddenly after being released, he joins them at the prayer meeting. If we were there, we might recall the promise of Christ, that on the rock (meaning the revelation of who Christ was) he would, through Peter, build his church. Thus, at the foundations of the early church, we find a living (prophetic) hope for the future. This future hope remains the critical foundational component for the building up of any local church, as well as the seed of prophetic destiny in the human heart.

> *Ephesians 2:19-20 Consequently, you are no longer foreigners and aliens, but fellow citizens with God's people and members of God's household, 20 built on the foundation of the apostles and prophets, with Christ Jesus himself as the chief cornerstone. NIV*

The anointing attendant with any ministry is like oil, which if poured on the head (leadership), saturates the body (local church). When a prophetic anointing is released into the church, a creative dynamism of revelatory dreams and insights are released into the rest of the body, producing amongst that body, a ripple effect. And so, when a prophet's anointing is released into a group of people, they also begin to get revelations.

We see this effect in the outpouring of the Spirit upon Saul and his men. When each of them came into contact with the company of prophets, they too began to prophesy, although they were soldiers

---

[14] 1 Corinthians 12:28 and in the church God has appointed first of all apostles, second prophets, third teachers, then workers of miracles, also those having gifts of healing, those able to help others, those with gifts of administration, and those speaking in different kinds of tongues. NIV

rather than prophets. The anointing upon the prophets was so strong that it rubbed off on Saul and his men.[15] Sometimes you have to travel to where the outpouring of the Holy Spirit is taking place to experience his effects.

> *"A prevailing and present anointing becomes a corporate one."*

This is one of God's strategies for bringing a corporate body into unity. In a similar fashion to what happened to Saul, once church members are touched with prophetic anointing oil; every member of the church can become a walking witness to outsiders, while moved by a communal grace, rather than just an individual gift.

If a community has a hunger for God and a strong relational bond, the release of a divine anointing into that community will result in an immediate impact. A similar outpouring was experienced by two of Moses' elders, Eldad and Medad, who received an anointing to prophesy when God poured it out on their peers, even though they

---

[15] *1 Samuel 19:19-24 Word came to Saul: "David is in Naioth at Ramah"; 20 so he sent men to capture him. But when they saw a group of prophets prophesying, with Samuel standing there as their leader, <u>the Spirit of God came upon Saul's men and they also prophesied.</u> 21 Saul was told about it, and he sent more men, and they prophesied too. <u>Saul sent men a third time, and they also prophesied</u>. 22 Finally, he himself left for Ramah and went to the great cistern at Secu. And he asked, "Where are Samuel and David?" "Over in Naioth at Ramah," they said. 23 <u>So Saul went to Naioth at Ramah. But the Spirit of God came even upon him, and he walked along prophesying until he came to Naioth</u>. 24 He stripped off his robes and also prophesied in Samuel's presence. He lay that way all that day and night. This is why people say, "Is Saul also among the prophets?" NIV*

were absent from the meeting at which the initial outpouring took place[16].

"Prophecies intended audience is first and foremost the church."

The prophetic voice is the key means by which a current dialogue with the church is entered into by God. But this does not mean that unbelievers cannot benefit from the experience, or that prophecy is only intended for the church. Israel, for example, was a prophetic statement for the nations.

I remember prophesying at a packed-out meeting in Kent. There must have been at least 40 non-Christians present at this evangelistic outreach. The church had worked very hard at inviting friends and families to this meeting, and after I had preached my heart out, I made an appeal, but no one responded. I looked towards heaven feeling disappointed that I had not adequately communicated the gospel. Instantly the Holy Spirit revealed the circumstance of one of the non-Christians who was present, how he had come to the meeting straight from an argument with his dad. As I described what the Lord was showing me the young man made his way out and stood in front of me. "That's me", he said, "I want to give myself to Jesus".

---

[16] *Numbers 11:26 However, two men, whose names were Eldad and Medad, had remained in the camp. They were listed among the elders, but did not go out to the Tent. Yet the Spirit also rested on them, and they prophesied in the camp. NIV*

This opened the door for many others who also came forward and responded for salvation.[17]

Because of all these benefits, prophecy is a gift which we are strongly encouraged to seek. It is to be permitted in every Christian enterprise. Organisations with corporate dreams pursue and accomplish incredible things, companies such as Microsoft or others like Nokia. How much more should organisations which have a divine revelation foster and encourage dreams that bring hope and command obedience. Such experience of prophecy makes our resolve firm and our heart strong. Our mind becomes fixed and steps, sure and energised.[18]

"Prophetic foundations establish a dynamic sense of destiny, direction and duty."

Coming back to the heart of worship, which is testifying to Christ and dispensing with trends and techniques as the means to bring us into relevance, gives us back our credibility with heaven. It answers the sincere desire of the church to be relevant, a relevance not found in a program, but in dialogue with heaven. Prophecy gives immediacy to that dialogue, changing church prayer meetings from being a one-way discourse and petition, to an engaging dialogue with heaven.

---

[17] *1 Corinthians 14:22-24 Tongues, then, are a sign, not for believers but for unbelievers; prophecy, however, is for believers, not for unbelievers. 23 So if the whole church comes together and everyone speaks in tongues, and some who do not understand or some unbelievers come in, will they not say that you are out of your mind? 24 But if an unbeliever or someone who does not understand comes in while everybody is prophesying, he will be convinced by all that he is a sinner and will be judged by all, NIV*

[18] *1 Corinthians 14:3 But everyone who prophesies speaks to men for their strengthening, encouragement and comfort. NIV*

Prophecy is a Window of Inspiration

FOUR-DIMENSIONAL INSPIRATION

If we understand life without prophetic inspiration to be like a painting, as two dimensional and flat, the only way to increase the depth of field is to split how the eyes see the image and introduce three-dimensional glasses, giving the illusion of three dimensions from a duplicated two-dimensional picture. The injection of prophetic content produces a four-dimensional effect in a three-dimensional world. Of course, it is altogether true that many things in life inspire. Many countless works of priceless art hang on august walls and in many a home simply because someone was inspired to paint it or inspired sufficiently to purchase it. Prophetic inspiration takes the individual into an altogether more complex tapestry. It makes life four-dimensional rather than three dimensional.

> *"Some great works of mathematics have come about by accident, but countless more breakthroughs by inspiration."*

Using another metaphor, I remember the first time that I used satellite navigation, and it was like having a sixth natural sense. From a little screen on my dashboard, I could not just see the layout of the road ahead of me, but all around. I knew what was coming, not because I had been there before, but because my little screen was like a prophetic window showing me what was ahead and even better, a nice ladylike voice would accurately tell me when to turn off or change lane. Travelling with satellite navigation was like having a bird's eye view on the future.

Other Worldly Vision.

The prophet is a seer as described in Hebrew, a *Ro'eh,* which means a seer,[19] someone able to acquire supernatural vision. The prophet was then able to receive from God, panoramic visions of supernatural dimensions not normally visible to men or angels.

This seeing ability of prophets helps us to understand why so many biblical prophecies are disseminated through picturesque language. For most people, the incredibly complicated visions of Daniel and the book of Revelation, instantly come to mind when considering prophecy. The idea that prophecy is meant to leave you in the dark, scratching your head, is not how we are intended to understand this precious gift. Impenetrable prophecy is not the norm or the aim. Even the book of Revelation is intended to be just that, a revelation to the reader. Therefore, we should approach prophecy with the attitude that God is seeking to communicate something pertinent to our lives and not to entertain the idea that he is seeking to confuse us.

---

[19] *1 Samuel 9:9 (Formerly in Israel, if a man went to inquire of God, he would say, "Come, let us go to the seer," because the prophet of today used to be called a seer.)*

The Prophet as an Eyewitness

Prophets are eyewitnesses, their confidence coming from personal experience rather than from handed down stories. The apostle Peter could never forget the amazing encounter he had with the glory of God on the mountain.[20] In that encounter, the distance between heaven and earth was clearly truncated when Moses and Elijah, who normally lived in heaven, also appeared on the mountain talking with Jesus. Indeed, the glory kept on increasing until it totally enveloped them all. As the glory presence increased, Jesus became translucent, sympathetically and wonderfully, reflecting his inner nature and glory.

Every true prophetic experience comes as a result of being in God's presence. Every such experience brings with it the chance for personal renewal, providing for the human heart an opportunity not always taken. For not every heart is hungry or seeking, but when we do encounter the manifest presence, we are left with a strong desire to do something to please God, to build altars of worship.[21] It would be better not to be impetuous in such circumstances and rather find the discipline to be still, resisting the temptation to take the initiative due to the increased spiritual ecstasy experienced. Rather we should wait for heaven's interpretation. When Peter found himself in this

---

[20] *2 Peter 1:16-18 (NIV) We did not follow cleverly invented stories when we told you about the power and coming of our Lord Jesus Christ, but we were eyewitnesses of his majesty. [17] For he received honour and glory from God the Father when the voice came to him from the Majestic Glory, saying, "This is my Son, whom I love; with him I am well pleased." [18] We ourselves heard this voice that came from heaven when we were with him on the sacred mountain.*

[21] *Matthew 17:1-5 (NIV) After six days Jesus took with him Peter, James and John the brother of James, and led them up a high mountain by themselves. [2] There he was transfigured before them. <u>His face shone like the sun</u>, and <u>his clothes became as white as the light</u>. [3] Just then there appeared before them Moses and Elijah, talking with Jesus. [4] Peter said to Jesus, "Lord, it is good for us to be here. If you wish, I will put up three shelters—one for you, one for Moses and one for Elijah."*

situation, he was encouraged to listen and not speak. A voice came out of the manifest glory giving direction.[22]

We know that wherever we see the glory, it represents the Father. Years later Peter recounts that experience, calling it a demonstration of Christ's majesty. The Father spoke then from manifest glory and continues to speak today from that same glory, particularly to those who come with childlike faith.[23] The moment we prefer to lean on our human wisdom rather than God's, we are in danger of remaining ignorant.

Jesus uses parables to encourage a humble approach to both how we relate to him and how we respond to the message he brought. The disciples who followed Christ had a real humility,[24] those who did not come in humility remained in the dark and often became his opponents.[25] The humble heart finds the secrets of heaven freely opened up; a hardened heart is unacceptable to God. Yet if one comes in humility, just as blind Bartimaeus and like him, reach out to Christ asking God for mercy, God will never walk past, because God

---

[22] *Matthew 17:5 While he was still speaking, a bright cloud enveloped them, and a voice from the cloud said, "This is my Son, whom I love; with him I am well pleased. Listen to him!" [6] When the disciples heard this, they fell facedown to the ground, terrified.*

[23] *Matthew 11:25-30 (NIV) At that time Jesus said, "I praise you, Father, Lord of heaven and earth, because you have hidden these things from the wise and learned, and revealed them to little children. [26] Yes, Father, for this was your good pleasure. [27] "All things have been committed to me by my Father. No one knows the Son except the Father, and no one knows the Father except the Son and those to whom the Son chooses to reveal him. [28] "Come to me, all you who are weary and burdened, and I will give you rest. [29] Take my yoke upon you and learn from me, for I am gentle and humble in heart, and you will find rest for your souls. [30] For my yoke is easy and my burden is light."*

[24] The Bondage of Pride - *Pride brings disgrace Pr 11:2;16:18; Pride deceives the heart Ob 1:3; Devalues others 1 Cor 4:6-7; Isa 37:23*

[25] *Matthew 13:10-15*

wants to speak to his children. The secrets and the wisdom of the kingdom are not meant to be a source of frustration and insecurity, but rather a source of spiritual knowledge and understanding for God's children.[26] By possessing this knowledge, we grow to be like the owner of a house filled with treasure[27], custodians of valuable but new insights, which the spirit willingly reveals.[28]

Seeing Experiences

Seeing experiences can come through dreams. Joseph had a seeing experience in a dream which had a profound impact upon his relationships.[29] Seeing his brothers and father bowing down to him in a prophetic dream, he could not curb his enthusiasm and joy as he

---

[26] *1 Corinthians 2:6-10 (NIV) We do, however, speak a message of wisdom among the mature, but not the wisdom of this age or of the rulers of this age, who are coming to nothing. [7] No, we speak of God's secret wisdom, a wisdom that has been hidden and that God destined for our glory before time began. [8] None of the rulers of this age understood it, for if they had, they would not have crucified the Lord of glory. [9] However, as it is written: "No eye has seen, no ear has heard, no mind has conceived what God has prepared for those who love him" — [10] but God has revealed it to us by his Spirit. The Spirit searches all things, even the deep things of God.*

[27] *Matthew 13:52 (NIV) He said to them, "Therefore every teacher of the law who has been **instructed** about the kingdom of heaven is like the owner of a house who brings out of his storeroom new treasures as well as old."*

[28] *Supernatural revelation comes by the Spirit - The believer prays in the Spirit (Ep 6:18; Jude 20); The spiritual man makes judgments about all things 1 Cor 2:15; The spirit will lead into truth John 16:15; Revelation can come in the context of worship 1 Cor 14:26; Always awaits the appointed time Hab 2:2-3; Requires a response Gal 2:2; General revelation is given to all Psa 19:1, Rom 1:19-20*

[29] *Genesis 37:5–10 (TEV) — 5 One night Joseph had a dream, and when he told his brothers about it, they hated him even more. 6 He said, "Listen to the dream I had. 7 We were all in the field tying up sheaves of wheat, when my sheaf got up and stood up straight. Yours formed a circle round mine and bowed down to it." 8 "Do you think you are going to be a king and rule over us?" his brothers asked. So they hated him even more because of his dreams and because of what he said about them. 9 Then Joseph had another dream and said to his brothers, "I had another dream, in which I saw the sun, the moon, and eleven stars bowing down to me." 10 He also told the dream to his father, and his father scolded him: "What kind of a dream is that? Do you think that your mother, your brothers, and I are going to come and bow down to you?"*

related his dream to them. His inability to contain what he saw was his Achilles heel, but unknown to him until many tears, challenges, temptations and anxieties later, this incredible gift to see the future in dreams would become the vehicle through which God was going to project him into his destiny.

Gideon received prophetic encouragement through someone else's dream, showing the diversity of such experiences. What he overheard gave him courage.[30] Gideon had to overcome so many personal fears and anxieties. He struggled, as many of us do, with personal insecurities. To be called by God to lead the war effort against an occupying force would have been a real challenge for anyone. But when he heard from the lips of his enemies a prophetic dream heralding his impending victory over them, he had the faith he needed to rise to the challenge.

The wise men of Babylon were similarly glad that Daniel had a seeing experience which enabled him to both know the content of, and the interpretation of Nebuchadnezzar's dream. A dream so terrifying it had filled the king with anxiety.[31] It was an anxiety that resulted in him ordering the execution of many of his closest spiritual advisers if they could not tell him the contents of his dream and the symbolic meaning of it.

---

[30] *Judges 7:13-15* **Gideon** *arrived just as a man was telling a friend his dream. "I had a dream," he was saying. "A round loaf of barley bread came tumbling into the Midianite camp. It struck the tent with such force that the tent overturned and collapsed." 14 His friend responded, "This can be nothing other than the sword of Gideon son of Joash, the Israelite. God has given the Midianites and the whole camp into his hands." 15 When Gideon heard the dream and its interpretation, he worshiped God. He returned to the camp of Israel and called out, "Get up! The LORD has given the Midianite camp into your hands." (NIV)*

[31] **Daniel** *2:1 In the second year of his reign, Nebuchadnezzar had dreams; his mind was troubled and he could not sleep. (C/f) Daniel 4:5 I had a dream that made me afraid. As I was lying in my bed, the images and visions that passed through my mind terrified me. (NIV)*

Seeing experiences can also come by visions. Normally when God spoke to a prophet he was wide awake, and so when Isaiah sees God sitting in court, filling the whole of heaven with his presence, he was cognizant of everything around him. One of my favourite prophetic stories is that of the encounter of Elisha and his servant at Dothan. Elisha could see more than his servant could at Dothan.[32] Although both were awake and watching the advancing army, only one of them had a vision in which he could see the marshalling forces of heaven; the other could not. At the point of prayer, Elisha's servant's eyes were opened, and the servant could see. Later on, because this servant never learned to submit, we find that he did not inherit the double portion of anointing he should have had from Elisha because he did not respect his master's injunction and disobeyed him. If he could not obey his earthly master who walked with God, how would he obey God?

Experiences Impact Theology

Experiences can be quite challenging and have an impact on how we understand scriptures. One morning the Lord asked the question, "which comes first, experience or theology?" It made me think; being a good, spirit filled, conservative, evangelical, everything within me wanted to scream "theology of course". Yet I was stumped because I realised that my earliest spiritual encounters with God were before I became a Christian. In my case experience won. David's experience of

---

[32] *2 Kings 6:16-18 "Don't be afraid," the prophet answered. "Those who are with us are more than those who are with them." 17 And Elisha prayed, "O LORD, open his eyes so he may see." Then the LORD opened the servant's eyes, and he looked and saw the hills full of horses and chariots of fire all around Elisha. 18 As the enemy came down toward him, Elisha prayed to the LORD, "Strike these people with blindness." So he struck them with blindness, as Elisha had asked. NIV*

Lessons *1. They were secure even though they were outnumbered, 2. God was not ignorant of the plight. 3. They were in command of the circumstances*

God led him under the inspiration of the Spirit to write Psalms about those experiences, which have in turn, become our scriptures. The lessons we learned through Job's sufferings might make us stop to ponder, but for him, they were real and painful experiences which he had to endure. The intention of the Lord asking me the question was to deliberately release me from religious strictures and invite me to enjoy life.

The scriptures are his word which he wants us to experience and read, not with a spirit of particular exactitude, but rather with the attitude of wonder and awe at this amazing God, who engages with the lives of those we read about. Allowing those scriptures to become my moral compass and the plumbline against which I measure and understand my life.

> *"Experience is the journey through which theology is understood."*

Whilst the scriptures remain our plumbline, what will it take to carry a prophetic message to the people of our day? How can we demonstrate what God looks like morally, spiritually, creatively and intellectually, through that prophetic lifestyle?

The challenges will require that we build on the experiences of our fathers and mothers and that we guard against becoming modern-day Pharisees, parrots who simply regurgitate what we have heard. And so, we need to be inspired by God.

As Father, it is his responsibility to inspire his children, to stretch them and cause them to grow intellectually, emotionally and spiritually. We may have a manual that tells us what to expect of a father, but better still is the experience of the tender love of an inspirational father, who puts flesh to understanding. He has something to say to us every day; a new experience to share with us, and this is the life of a prophet.

Seeing Mysteries

And so, our heavenly Father draws us into his throne room to gaze upon his beauty. He speaks to us of an eternity with him in a place so full of images of light that the mind struggles to grasp the magnitude of what God is preparing for us. Heaven is a place of wonder and mystery because God lives there. To see it is to catch a glimpse of how beautiful God is.[33] To see heaven is to see God, and as Ezekiel recounts his amazing experience,[34] we discover it to be an encounter filled with light. For Isaiah heaven is a place filled with the majesty of God, a temple of worship filled with his presence.[35]

When the prophets see; it is not just God that becomes visible, but the entourage that surrounds him, the "angels" of heaven[36], not just a few hundred, but tens of thousands multiplied by tens of thousands. Angelic beings of various sizes, abilities and with individual purpose surround God. Angels are seen to have indescribable features and unbelievable powers. When Father inspires us and opens our eyes to

---

[33] *Rev 21:1-22:7*

[34] *Ezekiel 1:28 (NIV) Like the appearance of a rainbow in the clouds on a rainy day, so was the radiance around him. This was the appearance of the likeness of the glory of the LORD. When I saw it, I fell facedown, and I heard the voice of one speaking.*

[35] *Isaiah 6:1 (NIV) In the year that King Uzziah died, I saw the Lord seated on a throne, high and exalted, and the train of his robe filled the temple.*

[36] *1 Kings 22:19 (NIV) Micaiah continued, "Therefore hear the word of the LORD: I saw the LORD sitting on his throne with all the host of heaven standing around him on his right and on his left.*

see, what we are left with is hard to describe and leaves us lost in wonder.

The throne of God is unlike any earthly throne; blazing with fire, able to transport itself to any point in time or space.[37] His throne is a throne of pure light and occupied by one who radiates light.[38] Jasper and carnelian,[39] a rainbow resembling an emerald, flashes of lightning, all emanate from the throne, and as if to ensure that enough light is shed, seven lamps, which are the seven spirits of God, are blazing. This is an amazing, spectacular display of glory; would two pairs of eyes be enough to take it all in? Heaven does not think so and so we find that the four living creatures are covered with eyes front, and back, two pairs of angelic eyes could never be enough to appreciate the beauty it beheld. What a vision, a throne set before a sea of glass clear as crystal, to ensure that every ray of light is perfectly mirrored.

We see because light enables sight; it allows the eyes to understand the world we occupy. True prophetic utterance is the result of

---

[37] *Daniel 7:9-10 (NIV) "As I looked, "thrones were set in place, and the Ancient of Days took his seat. His clothing was as white as snow; the hair of his head was white like wool. His throne was flaming with fire, and its wheels were all ablaze. [10] A river of fire was flowing, coming out from before him. Thousands upon thousands attended him; ten thousand times ten thousand stood before him. The court was seated, and the books were opened.*

[38] *Revelation 4:3-6 (NIV) And the one who sat there had the appearance of jasper and carnelian. A rainbow, resembling an emerald, encircled the throne. [4] Surrounding the throne were twenty-four other thrones, and seated on them were twenty-four elders. They were dressed in white and had crowns of gold on their heads. [5] From the throne came flashes of lightning, rumblings and peals of thunder. Before the throne, seven lamps were blazing. These are the seven spirits of God. [6] Also before the throne there was what looked like a sea of glass, clear as crystal. In the centre, around the throne, were four living creatures, and they were covered with eyes, in front and in back.*

[39] *Jasper and Carnelian are first and last gemstones worn on the high priests breast and Will be found in the foundations of the new Jerusalem*

spiritual light. To stand in the presence of God is to be spiritually illuminated inside and out. This is why the high priest wore a breastpiece with 12 gemstones. They were not just to represent the twelve tribes of Israel.

Picture the scene with me for just a minute. The high priest is coming out of the Holy of Holies; the Shekinah glory cloud is shining, what happens to the stones? Each one is radiating light; they seem alive with light, it appears that a river of light is flowing from the very inner being of the High Priest. Here is the prophetic narrative, to be illuminated you must stand in the presence of God. The prophetic eye sees because the light of God illuminates the darkness making the invisible visible.

God takes care not to expose us to more than we can bear. Too much light can destroy, as we see in the form of radiation. Intensely focused light can start a fire. God's pure glory is only revealed to us in manageable measures and what better way for God to protect us from the intensity of his glory, than to cover his glory with a cloud, just as he shields the earth with clouds to protect us from the intensity of the rays of the sun. To release a prophetic stream on earth is to invite God to illuminate us to enable us to see.

HEARING MYSTERIES

It is not just what we see that inspires; what we hear of the conversation in heaven is engaging. Its use of typology and metaphor, blurring symbolic with literal descriptions of the past, present and future; a mind and soul-stretching adventure.

As heaven becomes more audible and we learn to live in our Father's presence, the things that are heard are often hard to comprehend.

Ezekiel tries to describe the four living creatures, "cherubim", that he sees in heaven. They are seen to have four faces,[40] four wings, four sides, four sets of hands and one wheel. These angels form the chariot of God in a spiritual sense, transporting and guarding the throne of God. Interesting prophetic notes come through in the form of their visage, each sounding profound. For example, their four faces speak of their earthly function or global reach, as four is the number of the earth.[41]

The language of mystery is not intended to put us off this invitation into intimacy with the Father, nor is it designed to make it hard to grasp those things pertaining to his presence. Instead, mystery was designed to draw us in, and metaphoric language in its simplest form is used as an aid to help us understand, rather than to confuse. With a little patience, the metaphoric keys become clear, some blatantly obvious like the example given in scripture by Paul for physical training, which becomes a metaphor for spiritual discipline.[42] This helps us to understand the symbolism of the instruction.

The experience of heaven in its unabridged fullness is worth the pursuit; we are shown that it will be the enjoyment of a state of life without disease or "curse", a place of full and continuous employment.[43] This is not some "wearisome" work, for the effects of Adam's sin is fully removed.

---

[40] *Ezekiel 1:3-28*

[41] *[examples of 4 being the number of the earth]*

[42] *1 Timothy 4:8 (NIV) For physical training is of some value, but godliness has value for all things, holding promise for both the present life and the life to come.*

[43] *Revelation 22:3 (NIV) No longer will there be any curse. The throne of God and of the Lamb will be in the city, and his servants will serve him. (c/f) the tense here is future active i.e. his servants will keep on serving him*

EXPERIENCING WORSHIP

Worship is part of the language of heaven, a key component of renewal and the framework for a life lived in active relationship with the divine. Man longs for God's justice on the earth; the angels praise him, and through worship, magnify him for his perfect justice in heaven.[44] We are invited to step into this divine presence to enjoy what the angels enjoy, to see what they see and hear what they hear, in order that we might be able to worship like they worship.

Stepping into the Divine Presence

The apostle John did not hesitate to respond to the invitation to step into that spiritual place called heaven, where he was called up to witness future events.[45] Just like Jesus passing through the heavens,[46] John was exposed to wonderful sights of things invisible to the naked eye.

> *Hebrews 4:14 (NIV) Jesus the Great High Priest [14] Therefore, since we have a great high priest who has gone through the heavens, Jesus the Son of God, let us hold firmly to the faith we profess.*

---

[44] Revelation 19:1-3 (NIV) After this I heard what sounded like the roar of a great multitude in heaven shouting: "Hallelujah! Salvation and glory and power belong to our God, [2] <u>for true and just are his judgments</u>. He has condemned the great prostitute who corrupted the earth by her adulteries. He has avenged on her the blood of his servants." [3] And again they shouted: "Hallelujah! The smoke from her goes up for ever and ever."

[45] Revelation 4:1 (NIV) After this I looked, and there before me was a door standing open in heaven. And the voice I had first heard speaking to me like a trumpet said, "Come up here, and I will show you what must take place after this."

[46] Rabbis had a theology which spoke of seven heavens.

The apostle Paul also speaks about being caught up to what he called the third heaven.[47] He was prohibited, however, from revealing what he saw and heard. For not everything that is seen or heard in the divine presence is permitted to be revealed.[48] Paul warns that the loftiness of the experience is cause for caution. We must take great care not to become proud because of the visions we are being granted. To think too highly of oneself, due to heaven granting supernatural insight, is detrimental to the soul. At the same time, God wants us to celebrate and develop a sense of excitement and awe about the experiences he gives us and to share them with others, not as some badge of status, but as testimony to the consequence of relationship.

It is obviously clear that mention of a third heaven implies that there is a second[49] and a first heaven. Therefore we are drawn to inquire about the nature of such heavens, their locations, their purpose and

---

[47] *2 Co 12:1-9*

[48] *Genesis 37:5–10 (NKJV) — 5 Now Joseph had a dream, and he told it to his brothers; and they hated him even more. 6 So he said to them, "Please hear this dream which I have dreamed: 7 There we were, binding sheaves in the field. Then behold, my sheaf arose and also stood upright; and indeed your sheaves stood all around and bowed down to my sheaf." 8 And his brothers said to him, "Shall you indeed reign over us? Or shall you indeed have dominion over us?" So they hated him even more for his dreams and for his words. 9 Then he dreamed still another dream and told it to his brothers, and said, "Look, I have dreamed another dream. And this time, the sun, the moon, and the eleven stars bowed down to me." 10 So he told it to his father and his brothers; and his father rebuked him and said to him, "What is this dream that you have dreamed? Shall your mother and I and your brothers indeed come to bow down to the earth before you?"*

[49] *The first, could refer to the physical sky (Ho 2:18; Dan 7:13,), The second heaven could be the stellar spaces (cf. Ge 1:14-18). Or the abode of all supernatural angelic beings, The third heaven is the abode of the Triune God. Shamayi v'shamayim or the heaven of heavens, shamayim is plural*

Its location is unrevealed. It is the divine plan at present to populate the third heaven. It is a place of glory (Jn 14:1-3; Heb 2:10).

the promises they hold. Scripture does not describe specifically the first and second heaven.

Angelic Activity Accompanies Heaven

If we are to stand in the divine presence, we can expect the desire of Christ to become a common experience; "your kingdom come on earth as it is in heaven", we will no longer simply see into heaven, but find that heaven will manifest all around us; heaven coming to earth. I was once asked by a young believer what I thought about people who claim to have seen angels. My response probably surprised him, because I said that I had seen them myself, but had the good sense to be careful to whom, and how I shared my experiences because such experiences are outside the worldview of many fellow believers; consequentially some would simply not understand such manifestations. But, as heaven increasingly manifests in our lives, what else would we expect?

It should not surprise us that we have encounters with angels; you can't walk through a field and not encounter some grass, and you can't stand in the courts of heaven and not brush past angels as heaven has legions of them. In an increasing environment of ecstatic spirituality and a heightened sense of worship, we find ourselves mingling with this company who worship God in absolute purity. They dwell in a space in which God is greatly revered, perfectly honoured and enveloped by his limitless glory. Where such honour for God exists on earth, we can expect angels to encamp around those individuals.[50]

Nehemiah 9:6 (NIV) You alone are the LORD. You made the

---

[50] Psalms 34:7 (NIV) The angel of the LORD encamps around those who fear him, and he delivers them.

heavens, even the highest heavens, and all their starry host, the earth and all that is on it, the seas and all that is in them. You give life to everything, and the multitudes of heaven worship you.

Every believer has at least one angel assigned to watch over them, and probably more.[51] Christians have angelic guardians on a divine assignment to encourage the believer spiritually, fighting behind the scenes for the success of God's plan for their life.[52] These angels are lifelong guards. Those around Christ thought it normal to have angels visibly operating in their midst. When Peter was released from prison through angelic intervention, without the knowledge of his peers, it was thought more likely to have been his angel at the door rather than him in person. When Rhoda reported that he was at the door, it was met with incredulity that it could be him.[53]

But should we, in fact, speak to these angels? Whilst, the answer to this question could be shrouded in theological debate, Joseph, familiar with the presence and intervention of his angel, invoked blessings on his sons and called on his angel to do the same.[54] This was not identified in scripture as anything negative; of course, the

---

[51] *Matthew 18:10 (NIV) "See that you do not look down on one of these little ones. For I tell you that their angels in heaven always see the face of my Father in heaven.*

[52] *Angels are sent to serve inheritors Hebrews 1:14 (NIV)[14] Are not all angels ministering spirits sent to serve those who will inherit salvation?*

[53] *Acts 12:11-15 (NIV) [11] Then Peter came to himself and said, "Now I know without a doubt that the Lord sent his angel and rescued me from Herod's clutches and from everything the Jewish people were anticipating." [12] When this had dawned on him, he went to the house of Mary the mother of John, also called Mark, where many people had gathered and were praying. [13] Peter knocked at the outer entrance, and a servant girl named Rhoda came to answer the door. [14] When she recognized Peter's voice, she was so overjoyed she ran back without opening it and exclaimed, "Peter is at the door!" [15] "You're out of your mind," they told her. When she kept insisting that it was so, they said, "It must be his angel."*

[54] *Genesis 48:16 (NIV) the Angel who has delivered me from all harm —may he bless these boys. May they be called by my name and the names of my fathers Abraham and Isaac, and may they increase greatly upon the earth."*

bigger question is why would one want to dialogue with angels when we can speak to our Father directly rather than third-party intermediaries? Nevertheless, these wonderful angels surround us and aid us in mission. As they are sentient beings, as shown in scripture, they do from time to time dialogue with those they are sent to serve.

Many years ago, when Fiona and I first visited Kenya and stayed at a well-known Kenyan Missionary guest house, we met this amazing missionary who told us an astonishing story. He was initially called to work amongst the group of islands situated in Lake Victoria in Kenya. He recounted one story, in which missionaries were targeted by a group of occult practitioners. They threatened to get rid of him because the local witchdoctor, who also ran the local brewery, was not just losing money because of transformed lives, he was also losing adherents because they were becoming Christians. Since this particular missionary had arrived, people had stopped buying his alcohol and as far as the witchdoctor was concerned, it was time to summon up the spirits, beating his drums for over three nights to intimidate the missionary and his family. The native home help of the missionary decided to take a night off during this phase of the beating of the drums, because whilst the new missionary did not know it, the home help knew that the witchdoctor and his cronies were going to attack the missionary's home on that particular night.

The next day he came rushing back to tell the missionary that something extraordinary had happened the previous night. He explained to the missionary the real reason why he and other native workers on the island had signed off work the previous night. He then went on to explain that when the witchdoctor's henchmen approach the island, they saw a vast number of men who were seven feet tall and glowing white, lining the shore. The witchdoctor and his henchmen were terrified and turned back. Apparently, these men circled the whole of the island. This resulted in the witchdoctor himself surrendering his life to Christ and confessing to everyone who would listen, what had happened.

When I was preaching in our local church on the manifestation of angels being a consequence of the presence of heaven, one of our members told me a story of an encounter with angels at spring harvest, a national Christian camp. She saw the angels but did not really realise what they were. She just saw bright lights amongst the children who were being taken from one meeting to another. It was the children who alerted adults to what was going on when the children wanted to know who the bright men were that were walking amongst them.

We would certainly expect heightened angelic activity at key junctions in our lives.[55]

For a prophet, this is a key consideration. The forces of heaven are marshalled to execute his will because prophetic activity is done in the harshest of environments in a world full of not just fallen people but fallen angels.[56]

---

[55] *In the Life of Christ Angelic intervention is revealed in key moments. Angel from heaven rolled stone away Mat 28:2-4, Their clothes white as snow, Their appearance like lightening*

[56] *Luke 10:18 (NIV) [18] He replied, "I saw Satan fall like lightning from heaven. (c/f) Isaiah 14:12-13 (NIV) [12] How you have fallen from heaven, O morning star, son of the dawn! You have been cast down to the earth, you who once laid low the nations! [13] You said in your heart, "I will ascend to heaven; I will raise my throne above the stars of God; I will sit enthroned on the mount of assembly, on the utmost heights of the sacred mountain.*

INSPIRATIONAL CHARACTERS

Inspired Prophets

Those who gave prophecy were regarded as *Nabiy* . The Hebrew word *'nabiy'* means inspired man. A work of the Holy Spirit through which he gives the prophet ecstatic utterance.[57] Once inspired, their feats and lives in turn, became inspiring. The word nabiy first appeared in Genesis, speaking about Abraham. Once God had spoken to him, he became inspired to leave his home and set out on an adventure to a new land and make it his home. He obeyed even though he was unsure about the destination.[58] Despite the dangers en-route, he depended on God to rescue him when help was needed and to guide him when direction was required.[59]

Abraham's journey was not a man-induced gold rush as happened during the California Gold Rush of 1849, but rather the journey of a man based on a promise by God. It is true that he was offered an inheritance for both him and his descendants, but the reason for his departure was obedience and relationship with a God, in whom he had put his faith.

Moses was inspired right from his first meeting with God on the mountain; noticing the miraculous bush which did not burn up. It is

---

[57] 2 Peter 1:21 *For prophecy never had its origin in the will of man, but men spoke from God as they were carried along by the Holy Spirit. (NIV).*

[58] Hebrews 11:8 *By faith Abraham, when called to go to a place he would later receive as his inheritance, obeyed and went, even though he did not know where he was going. (NIV).*

[59] Genesis 20:7 *Now return the man's wife, for he is a prophet, and he will pray for you and you will live. But if you do not return her, you may be sure that you and all yours will die." (C/f) Psalms 105:15 "Do not touch my anointed ones; do my prophets no harm."(NIV).*

interesting to think that Father needs to attract our attention, that he uses unusual methods to draw us closer to him. For Moses, this was the start of an exciting adventure, with God commanding him to perform the miracles and plagues before Pharaoh. He not only continued to be inspired himself, nor did he only become an inspiration to the people of God trapped as slaves in Egypt, but over the centuries his exploits continue to inspire us. He came to the slaves in Egypt, with God's word burning in his mouth[60] and when we listen to what he had to say, his prophetic words still burn in our hearts today. God granted him an extraordinary prophetic gifting so accurate and so precise that Pharaoh would feel like God was standing before him.

> *Exodus 7:1-2 Then the LORD said to Moses, "See, I have made you like God to Pharaoh, and your brother Aaron will be your prophet. 2 You are to say everything I command you, and your brother Aaron is to tell Pharaoh to let the Israelites go out of his country."*

Prophecy does not just come to adults; Samuel was another inspirational prophet familiar with prophetic revelation from his earliest childhood.[61] I have to laugh at the notion that children are not very spiritual when scripture repeatedly points out the opposite.

---

[60] *Deuteronomy 18:18 I will raise up for them a prophet like you from among their brothers; I will put my words in his mouth, and he will tell them everything I command him. (C/f) Hosea 12:13 The LORD used a prophet to bring Israel up from Egypt, by a prophet he cared for him. (C/f) Numbers 11:25 Then the LORD came down in the cloud and spoke with him, and he took of the Spirit that was on him and put the Spirit on the seventy elders. When the Spirit rested on them, they prophesied, but they did not do so again. (C/f) Numbers 12:2 "Has the LORD spoken only through Moses?" they asked. "Hasn't he also spoken through us?" And the LORD heard this.*

[61] ***1 Samuel 3:1–4 (TEV)** — **1** In those days, when the boy Samuel was serving the LORD under the direction of Eli, there were very few messages from the LORD, and visions from him were quite rare. **2** One night Eli, who was now almost blind, was sleeping in his own room; **3** Samuel was sleeping in the sanctuary, where the sacred Covenant Box was. Before dawn, while the lamp was still burning, **4** the LORD called Samuel. He answered, "Yes, sir!"*

Indeed, age is not an indicator of spirituality. Samuel had special administrative gifting demonstrated by the fact that under his guidance prophecy became more organised amongst those serving Yahweh.[62] Contemporary attempts to bring similar structure to prophecy is to be applauded, just as iron sharpens iron, in a school of prophets each prophetic gifting sharpens the others and illuminates the community, much in the same way as we see the Old Testament school of prophets bringing the word of the Lord to the nation. Such schools of prophecy were organised in order that the word of the Lord might be accessible to the people.

From this organisational approach, we gather that teams of people who heard the voice of God worked well together, giving us insight into how true worship is often central to the prophetic experience and enhances prophetic ecstasy. Whilst in our current age we may focus more on David's kingly ministry, in Old Testament times he was not just considered a king, but also thought of as a prophet who expressed his prophetic gifting primarily through music, similar to the sanctuary singers who prophesied in the course of their service to Yahweh.[63]

Worship has always been an instrument through which inspirational prophecy is released and inspired. It is said that in the course of temple worship, the priests experienced dozens of miracles every day. Amazing signs, wonders and miracles did not just accompany

---

[62] *1 Samuel 10:5 "After that you will go to Gibeah of God, where there is a Philistine outpost. As you approach the town, you will meet a procession of prophets coming down from the high place with lyres, tambourines, flutes and harps being played before them, and they will be prophesying.*

[63] *1 Chronicles 25:3 As for Jeduthun, from his sons: Gedaliah, Zeri, Jeshaiah, Shimei, Hashabiah and Mattithiah, six in all, under the supervision of their father Jeduthun, who prophesied, using the harp in thanking and praising the LORD.*

prophets like Elijah but were also performed as part of the organised company of prophets.[64]

---

[64] *2 kings 6:1-7*

Prophetic Accuracy Produces Confidence

Great care must be exercised in the receipt of a prophecy, as all prophecies have to be weighed and tested.[65] Reluctance to open up a prophecy to the scrutiny of others could be a signal of delusion, insecurity or even illness. The patient individual, taking time to weigh up a prophetic word, does not signal a lack of faith, but rather the wisdom of a son seeking to understand the instructions of a Father. The mechanism for weighing prophecy is clear in the scriptures, and so we can focus on that, which once weighed is found to be genuine.[66]

Any study on prophecy very quickly unearths the incredible accuracy of prophecies in the scriptures. With a high degree of confidence, the church or individual can structure their entire life, or give their resources to the fulfilment of received prophecy, knowing that they

---

[65] **1 Corinthians 14:29 (NIV)** — **29** Two or three prophets should speak, and the others should weigh carefully what is said.

[66] *How to weigh up prophecy - if present others with a prophetic gift should weigh the prophetic word - 1 Corinthians 14:26–33 (ESV)* — *26 What then, brothers? When you come together, each one has a hymn, a lesson, a revelation, a tongue, or an interpretation. Let all things be done for building up. 27 If any speak in a tongue, let there be only two or at most three, and each in turn, and let someone interpret. 28 But if there is no one to interpret, let each of them keep silent in church and speak to himself and to God. 29 Let two or three prophets speak, and let the others weigh what is said. 30 If a revelation is made to another sitting there, let the first be silent. 31 For you can all prophesy one by one, so that all may learn and all be encouraged, 32 and the spirits of prophets are subject to prophets. 33 For God is not a God of confusion but of peace. As in all the churches of the saints,*

are not wasting their talents. We will look at three historical examples of just how accurate prophecy can be.

> *"The prophetically structured life need not rely on hindsight."*

The Accuracy of the Prophecy Concerning Tyre.

We cannot afford to miss out the incredible prophetic word spoken over Tyre in 586 BC. Tyre, a great seafaring nation, was to be completely destroyed and the whole city, every boulder, beam and roof tile was to be thrown into the sea.

Although the language of the prophecy looks metaphorical, it was, in fact, going to be a literal experience. Tyre had become proud and was revelling in Jerusalem's difficulties, seeing Jerusalem's struggles as an opportunity to become rich, and so God speaks to Tyre.

> *Ezekiel 26:1–5 (ESV) — 1 In the eleventh year, on the first day of the month, the word of the LORD came to me: 2 "Son of man, because Tyre said concerning Jerusalem, 'Aha, the gate of the peoples is broken; it has swung open to me. I shall be replenished, now that she is laid waste,' 3 therefore thus says the Lord GOD: Behold, I am against you, O Tyre, and will bring up many nations against you, as the sea brings up its waves. 4 They shall destroy the walls of Tyre and break down her towers, and I will scrape her soil from her and make her a bare rock. 5 She shall be in the midst of the sea a place for the spreading of nets, for I have spoken, declares the Lord GOD. And she shall become plunder for the nations,*

There is non-literal language used to indicate the relentlessness of God's impending judgment over the city. It was going to come "like the sea churning up its waves", but the outcomes and approaching events were going to be literal. We will look at two of the 'waves' connected with this prophecy. The first wave was going to be the incursion of Babylon led by Nebuchadnezzar. He was to come and build up siege works and attack the city.

> *Ezekiel 26:6–8 (ESV) — 6 and her daughters on the mainland shall be killed by the sword. Then they will know that I am the LORD. 7 "For thus says the Lord GOD: Behold, I will bring against Tyre from the north Nebuchadnezzar king of Babylon, king of kings, with horses and chariots, and with horsemen and a host of many soldiers. 8 He will kill with the sword your daughters on the mainland. He will set up a siege wall against you and throw up a mound against you and raise a roof of shields against you.*

Nebuchadnezzar fulfilled this part of the prophecy between 587-573 with Nebuchadnezzar's 13-year siege of Tyre, which ended in 572 forever weakening Phoenician national life and power. Fulfilment of the second and most amazing wave of this prophecy is astonishing. Old Tyre was never to be inhabited again. She was to become a bare rock, and all her fine houses were to be thrown into the sea.

> *Ezekiel 26:12–17 (ESV) — 12 They will plunder your riches and loot your merchandise. They will break down your walls and destroy your pleasant houses. Your stones and timber and soil they will cast into the midst of the waters. 13 And I will stop the music of your songs, and the sound of your lyres shall be heard no more. 14 I will make you a bare rock. You shall be a place for the spreading of nets. You shall never be rebuilt, for I am the LORD; I have spoken, declares the Lord GOD. 15 "Thus says the Lord GOD to Tyre: Will not the coastlands shake at the sound of your fall, when the wounded groan, when slaughter is made in your midst? 16 Then all the princes of the sea will step down from their thrones and remove their robes and strip off their embroidered garments. They will clothe themselves with trembling; they will sit on the ground and tremble every moment and be appalled at you. 17 And they will raise a lamentation over you and say to you, " How you have perished, you who were inhabited from the seas, O city renowned, who was mighty on the sea; she and her inhabitants imposed their terror on all her inhabitants!*

The fulfilment came in July 332 B.C. when Alexander the Great conquered Tyre[67]. Alexander the Great had been marching south against the Persian empire. On approaching Tyre, he was not given permission to enter the city, and the Tyrians decided to kill a party of heralds sent to negotiate a peace treaty. Because the city had an island fortress and due to their reliance on support which they expected to come from Carthage, with which they had a bond, they were confident of being able to resist Alexander.

In addition to this confidence, Alexander's entire navy was too far away to give immediate assistance. It eventually took Alexander six months with the aid of his ships and the building of a dam to take the island fortress. In the process, the Tyrian navy was destroyed, and he had 2,000 of them impaled on the walls and sold 20,000 into slavery

The fulfilment of what could have been understood to be purely picturesque language came because Alexander the Great needed materials with which to build the breakwater in order that he might reach the island fortress. The handiest materials were the buildings and general infrastructure of Tyre itself. So, he literally levelled Tyre and used every stone of the city to build his breakwater, literally scraping the city from the face of the map (Ezek 26:4).

Taken at face value this prophecy would have seemed non-literal, but the opposite was true. Therefore, we need to be careful not to assume that the language of the OT is simply metaphoric picture language, intended to convey truth and nothing else. There are many examples of non-literal prophetic utterances, but prophetic pictures should never be simply dismissed in the first instance as non-literal

---

[67] *the detailed of which are described by two ancient historians: Arrian and Quintus Curtius Rufus*

unless scripture itself explains that they are not, or to take it as such would be ridiculous.

The Accuracy of David's Revelation of the Crucifixion

The prophecy of David provides an excellent first example. In Psalm 22, which was written hundreds of years before Christ was born, we find David prophetically describing the crucifixion of the Christ. It starts with the final moments that Christ was to experience on the cross.

> *Psalm 22:1–2 (ESV) — 1 My God, my God, why have you forsaken me? Why are you so far from saving me, from the words of my groaning? 2 O my God, I cry by day, but you do not answer, and by night, but I find no rest.*

Jesus said these very words in Matthew 27:46 "Eloi, Eloi, lama sabachthani?"- which means, "My God, my God, why have you forsaken me?" This was a direct quotation of a prophecy. The Christ had a profound sense of son-ship, he knew who he was. The cry which could be read as rejection could equally be the affirmation of prophetic knowledge, a declaration of being right in the centre of God's will, whilst at the same time not implying any detraction from the real sense of anguish and isolation he felt on the cross. Any suggestion that this equates to a lack of faith or trust in God his Father, must be resisted. We find that David continues in this Psalm to explain events he saw surrounding the suffering of the Messiah. He could see the mocking of Christ on the cross.[68]

> *Psalm 22:14–18 (ESV) — 14 I am poured out like water, and*

---

[68] Psalm 22:6–8 (ESV) — 6 But I am a worm and not a man, scorned by mankind and despised by the people. 7 All who see me mock me; they make mouths at me; they wag their heads; 8 "He trusts in the LORD; let him deliver him; let him rescue him, for he delights in him!"

all my bones are out of joint; my heart is like wax; it is melted within my breast; 15 my strength is dried up like a potsherd, and my tongue sticks to my jaws; you lay me in the dust of death. 16 For dogs encompass me; a company of evildoers encircles me; they have pierced my hands and feet— 17 I can count all my bones— they stare and gloat over me; 18 they divide my garments among them, and for my clothing they cast lots. Other accurate details, which are unveiled in the Psalm, are the predictions that his hands and feet would be pierced, that he would experience thirst[9] on the cross and that his oppressors would cast lots for his clothes.

The Accuracy of Jesus' Prophecies about Jerusalem

Jesus prophesied that Jerusalem would be left desolate.[70] Concerning the temple, he said not one stone would be left on another.[71] This was fulfilled when the Roman General, Titus, ordered his soldiers to dig up the very foundations of the temple as predicted by Micah.[72] The temple area would be made so flat it could be ploughed like a field. Josephus, the historian, affirmed that the temple was so level that no one visiting the city would believe it had been inhabited.[73] It was first predicted that this would happen by Jeremiah, but the Lord

---

[69] John 19:28–30 (ESV) — 28 After this, Jesus, knowing that all was now finished, said (to fulfil the Scripture), "I thirst." 29 A jar full of sour wine stood there, so they put a sponge full of the sour wine on a hyssop branch and held it to his mouth. 30 When Jesus had received the sour wine, he said, "It is finished," and he bowed his head and gave up his spirit.

[70] Matthew 23:37–38 (ESV) — 37 "O Jerusalem, Jerusalem, the city that kills the prophets and stones those who are sent to it! How often would I have gathered your children together as a hen gathers her brood under her wings, and you were not willing! 38 See, your house is left to you desolate.

[71] Matthew 24:2 (ESV) — 2 But he answered them, "You see all these, do you not? Truly, I say to you, there will not be left here one stone upon another that will not be thrown down."

[72] Micah 3:12 (ESV) — 12 Therefore because of you Zion shall be plowed as a field; Jerusalem shall become a heap of ruins, and the mountain of the house a wooded height.

[73] JOSEPHUS, The Jewish War

postponed it because Micah and Isaiah convinced Hezekiah to repent.[74]

> *Jeremiah 26:18–19 (ESV)* — 18 *"Micah of Moresheth prophesied in the days of Hezekiah king of Judah, and said to all the people of Judah: 'Thus says the LORD of hosts, " 'Zion shall be plowed as a field; Jerusalem shall become a heap of ruins, and the mountain of the house a wooded height.' 19 Did Hezekiah king of Judah and all Judah put him to death? Did he not fear the LORD and entreat the favor of the LORD, and did not the LORD relent of the disaster that he had pronounced against them? But we are about to bring great disaster upon ourselves."*

Jesus predicted that the judgment referred to would still affect Jerusalem and that she would have an embankment built that would encircle her.[75] The word used is *charaka*, the singular form *charak* means pointed stake. Josephus tells us that in 3 days the invading Roman army built a high wall of earth, held in place by pointed stakes around the whole city. Jerusalem was to be trodden down by the gentiles until the time of the gentiles was fulfilled.[76] Scripture shows us that the temple is not going to be rebuilt until the time of the gentiles is fulfilled.

> *Luke 21:6–8 (ESV)* — 6 *"As for these things that you see, the days will come when there will not be left here one stone upon another that will not be thrown down." 7 And they asked him, "Teacher, when will these things be, and what will be the sign when these things are about to take place?" 8 And he said, "See that you are not led astray. For many will come in my name, saying, 'I am*

---

[74] Isa 37:33-37

[75] Luke 19:43 The days will come upon you when your enemies will build an embankment against you and encircle you and hem you in on every side. NIV

[76] Luke 21:24 They will fall by the sword and will be taken as prisoners to all the nations. Jerusalem will be trampled on by the Gentiles until the times of the Gentiles are fulfilled. NIV

he!' and, 'The time is at hand!' Do not go after them.

We are told in history that Julian, called the apostate nephew of Constantine, who tried to revive paganism, decided to restore the Jews and rebuild the temple to show Jesus was a false prophet. In 363, Julian, on his way to engage Persia, stopped at the ruins of the second temple in Jerusalem. In keeping with his effort to foster religions other than Christianity, Julian ordered the temple rebuilt. A personal friend of his, Ammianus Marcellinus, wrote this about the effort:

> *"Julian thought to rebuild at an extravagant expense the proud Temple once at Jerusalem, and committed this task to Alypius of Antioch. Alypius set vigorously to work, and was seconded by the governor of the province; when fearful balls of fire, breaking out near the foundations, continued their attacks, till the workmen, after repeated scorching, could approach no more: and he gave up the attempt."*

God's divine intervention was believed at the time to be the reason for his failure. Secularly, this failure to rebuild the temple was put down to earthquakes, whirlwinds and eruptions which made it impossible.

Prophecy Stimulates Renewal

Even where discouragement has settled in, God can use such accurately placed prophecy to revive a person or a people who are in danger of becoming spiritually cold, and he uses past fulfilment to re-establish them in divine purpose. We know that through the prophetic gift there is always the opportunity for a second chance because prophecy is often shrouded in the conditional "if".[77] An open door to reconnect with the divine will.

"Prophecy is a channel for revival and a catalyst for new life."

The Lord can take an old prophecy and apply it to a new situation, and the recipients will find it is no less accurate. So, in the case of the prophecy against Tyre, prophecy can have more than one application and more than one time-frame to which it refers. The dry bones of Ezekiel 37 are not the first time God has made bones live. He created a whole human out of one single bone.[78]

He comes back again to the theme of bones in the Book of Ezekiel. God can use a prophetic word and apply it to many situations. For example, the victory of Ezekiel's prophecy in chapter 37 can be applied in various ways by the Holy Spirit to various situations or peoples as he so chooses. It can be applied to Israel's resurrection, it can be applied to the resurrection of the soul from death,[79] and it can be applied to the resurrection of a family church ligament by ligament, individual to individual. It can be applied to a prophetic word received in the past which now seems dead but comes alive

---

[77] *2 Chronicles 7:14 (ESV) — 14 if my people who are called by my name humble themselves, and pray and seek my face and turn from their wicked ways, then I will hear from heaven and will forgive their sin and heal their land.*

[78] *Genesis 2:21–23 (ESV) — 21 So the LORD God caused a deep sleep to fall upon the man, and while he slept took one of his ribs and closed up its place with flesh. 22 And the rib that the LORD God had taken from the man he made into a woman and brought her to the man. 23 Then the man said, "This at last is bone of my bones and flesh of my flesh; she shall be called Woman, because she was taken out of Man."*

[79] *John 5:23-25*

again to the recipient. It can be applied to the resurrection of a dead ministry because even in death, some bones still carry an anointing.[80]

---

[80] *2 Kings 13:21*

Prophecy Aligns our Will with Heaven

When we look at the life of the biblical prophets it challenges how we currently live. If they could display such extraordinary powers, then what kind of powers should those who have inherited eternal life and are filled with the power of the Holy Spirit display? By virtue of the relationship we have with our Father in heaven, we should demonstrate similarly extraordinary lives.

I recall a dream I had during a period of between 18 months and two years[81] when God woke me up early every morning and spoke to me. Sometimes he would give me dreams, sometimes visions. In one dream the Lord spoke to me showing me a vision of trees all reflecting his glory. Now those who know me, know that when I preach, I sometimes mix up my metaphors. In this dream, the Lord said to me "people cannot see the trees for the wood".

I immediately wanted to correct the Lord and point out to him that what he meant to say was that people couldn't see the wood for the trees. And then the Lord said it again "people cannot see the trees for the wood", this time I listened, and the Lord said to me in the dream, "Yinka people see the trees and don't recognise the glory of my

---

[81] 2008-2010

creation. Rather than see what I have done, when people look at the trees, they think about the planks of wood and what they can make from the trees. Yet the trees carry a glory because they were formed by my hands." Then the Lord said something which shocked me, he said "Yinka I don't mind what people create with the planks of wood as long as I'm the glory at the centre of what they are building, I really don't care about religion as long as I am truly the object and at the centre of it."

Now at this point, I had two struggles. The first being the recognition of the constructs I have made with my own hands in which God, whilst not absent, was not really the focal point. The other problem I had was that I now had to grapple with the idea that God doesn't mind religion and that he is just opposed to religion that doesn't have him at the centre of it. When I woke up, I had a long theological discussion with the Lord, and he helped me get rid of some religious attitudes.

To demonstrate supernatural lifestyles, we will invariably have to rid ourselves of religious attitudes that have nothing to do with a relationally motivated gospel. If anything, those prophets of the Old Testament had a relationship with God who directed their ministries. And now, just as then, there are those whose ministries are not so much inspired by God, as by religion. Of course, it is easy to build ministries and retrospectively convince oneself that it has the hallmark of God upon it.

Many have tried to make the kingdom a function of their works; revising theologically what the kingdom is, to suit the obvious good works they are engaged in. The ultimate test for me now is how these "kingdom works" genuinely relate to, and are covered by, local church leadership. We know that as part of the call to bring glory to God, believers must, in the pursuit of the kingdom, demonstrate good works.[82] A few ground rules will help us in our discernment of what is truly meant by the word kingdom. Jesus makes clear his kingdom is not of this world.[83]

The key to finally helping me grasp this was a message I heard from Colin Urquhart, who pointed out that Jesus made the kingdom an issue of internal lifestyle and attitude, rather than manifest organisations and structures. Such thinking removes the temptation of a political agenda. He makes it clear it is about integrity of relationship with heaven rather than works.[84] For Colin Urquhart, the kingdom is about how we live with the seven principles of mercy, love, increase, faith, authority, power and unity. I found it fascinating because he did not make the kingdom a function of our works, but rather a question of how heaven shapes our character.

This is the demarcation line between religion and life! This is the kingdom that Christ wants us to draw down, one which enforces, through a personally submitted life, the will of God down here on earth. Just as the life of God is seen up in heaven, by demonstrating a submitted life to the will of the Father we will see the life of heaven down here on earth.

---

[82] *Matthew 6:9–13 (GNT) — 9 This, then, is how you should pray: 'Our Father in heaven: May your holy name be honored; 10 may your Kingdom come; may your will be done on earth as it is in heaven. 11 Give us today the food we need. 12 Forgive us the wrongs we have done, as we forgive the wrongs that others have done to us. 13 Do not bring us to hard testing, but keep us safe from the Evil One.'*

[83] *John 8:36 (GNT) — 36 If the Son sets you free, then you will be really free.*

[84] *Luke 17:20 (GNT) — 20 Some Pharisees asked Jesus when the Kingdom of God would come. His answer was, "The Kingdom of God does not come in such a way as to be seen.*

Jesus encourages the use of the framework of prayer to both access and guide us in God's will. It is to the Father that he encourages us to pray and through prayer to enforce the will of God on earth because ***prayer draws heaven down to earth.*** This is the essence of the prophetic voice, which like Christ, hears what the Father is saying and through prayer meditates on it.

Christ is saying that the Father cares, speak to him directly and he will give you what you ask.[85] This invitation to pray is the means through which Christ enforces the bridgehead between heaven and earth. As we engage in drawing the Father into our circumstances, we are in fact drawing heaven down to earth. And through our humble submission, we are facilitating an expression of God's rule and reign on the earth.[86]

Worship produces a similar effect to the one produced by prayer because worship also draws heaven down to earth. Believers, by virtue of the fact that they are heavenly citizens, are able to step into the heavenly arena of worship, they are able to approach the Father and like the angels, proclaim him holy.[87] Through that eternal bridge called the cross, this sense of being able to access the Father's throne

---

[85] *Jeremiah 3:19 (GNT) — 19 The LORD says, "Israel, I wanted to accept you as my child and give you a delightful land, the most beautiful land in all the world. I wanted you to call me father, and never again turn away from me.*

[86] *Kingdom It is best to understand this kingdom as having present existence through the church, the body of Christ. Although Jesus himself is physically resident in heaven (Ac 1:11; Col 4:1), he is vitally and truly present in the members of his body here on earth.   When and if we are obedient to divine will, we represent the continuing direct breakthrough of the spiritual realm into the material: we represent the kingdom of heaven on earth. Heaven is now timeless and locationless for the believer living in the Spirit.*

[87] *"hallowed" as in hallowed be your name means is the Greek word Hagiazo meaning to make holy or to be consecrated .*

room at any point in time is also a legal state of grace gifted to believers.

The cross ensures there is no distance between the worshipers in heaven and the worshipers on earth. We can all stand in the holy of holies. This dual activity of reverent worship and petitioning prayer solicits the governance of heaven in our lives. Effectively making Christ Lord.

"Heaven is where we are now seated and from where we are now ruled"

On earth, his control is indirect; a control that some, including fallen angels, vigorously oppose. The contrast with heaven cannot be clearer. In heaven, everyone's will is joyfully subject to God's own will they are perfectly governed by heaven. When we pray "your kingdom come, your will be done on earth as it is in heaven", we are asking for the perfection of his will in our lives, just as is seen in heaven, requiring total surrender and total dependency for the most basic of needs; a truly prophetic walk. For when we pray "give us today our daily bread", we are making a faith statement. The exercise of faith becomes another route through which we can materialise its benefits on earth, and through which practical heavenly provision can be received.

This prophetic message about heaven demands a change in character that goes beyond a superficial response. When we pray "forgive us our sins", we indeed show personal humility, but when we "forgive those who sinned against us", we are, through our act of charity, prophesying the mercy[88] of God. The lifestyle lived, which

---

[88] *Eph 4:32; Mat 18:28-30*

encapsulates and then mirrors this tender heart of God, clearly shows more light than many humanly motivated good works. This bridgehead between heaven and earth will ultimately result in the glory of God being revealed. Christ reveals to us that the kingdom belongs to the Father, and the glory belongs to him.[89]

There are times when God chooses to self-manifest that glory in scripture, and so we read about the glory cloud manifesting. The glory cloud always speaks to us about the presence of the Father and so in scripture, when you see the glory cloud, you are witnessing revelation about both the person of the Father and those things which accompany a manifestation of his presence. The route and means through which we best manifest and reflect the Lord's glory is not dissimilar to both Moses and our saviour, meaning it requires both intimate personal relationship in the presence and total submission to his will.

The Spiritual Realm is the Location of our True Life and our Hope.

To be in Christ then is to be citizens of heaven,[90] a spiritual realm. Our right to live as a citizen of heaven has been secured by Christ. One day we will fully experience heaven, but we are also a part of that glorious place called heaven now. Our names bear testimony to that fact, as they are already recorded in the books of heaven.[91] If the mindset

---

[89] *Mat 5:37*

[90] *Philippians 3:20 (GNT) — 20 We, however, are citizens of heaven, and we eagerly wait for our Saviour, the Lord Jesus Christ, to come from heaven.*

[91] *Luke 10:20 (GNT) — 20 But don't be glad because the evil spirits obey you; rather be glad because your names are written in heaven." (c/f) Hebrews 12:23 (GNT) — 23 You have come to the joyful gathering of God's firstborn, whose names are written in heaven. You have come to God, who is the judge of all people, and to the spirits of good people made perfect.*

under which we labour is restricted in its understanding of the spiritual privileges and opportunities we now possess, then we will live under temporal laws, which blinker a fuller understanding not fully deploying the privileges granted to us. But if we understand that our citizenship is from above, we will live as if we have access to the throne room above. Old Testament prophets gazed into this heavenly throne room as bystanders, watching in a sense from afar. Theirs was not the benefit of sonship; they could not sit with him in the heavenly places, a privilege afforded to us as sons and daughters.

I remember the first time I, as a black man, was called a "white man" by a group of Ghanaian children; it was rather amusing. I was leading a team from England, the team was made up of Caucasians except myself, and the children just saw me as being the same as the other white English team members, even though I was just as black as the Ghanaian children calling me a white man. A powerful metaphor that we end up looking the same as those we spend time with. Our lives can look the same as the lives of those who presently dwell with God. As I said in my book *Personal Transformation*, "if you live in a place long enough, you develop characteristics that mark you out as coming from that place".

Because our citizenship is in heaven, we are governed[92] by better laws. It is not in the political material realm of earth, but in the theocratic spiritual realm of heaven that our true wealth[93] and reward

---

[92] *Galatians 4:26 (GNT) — 26 But the heavenly Jerusalem is free, and she is our mother.; Hebrews 12:22 (GNT) — 22 Instead, you have come to Mount Zion and to the city of the living God, the heavenly Jerusalem, with its thousands of angels.; Revelation 21:2 (GNT) — 2 And I saw the Holy City, the new Jerusalem, coming down out of heaven from God, prepared and ready, like a bride dressed to meet her husband.*

[93] *Matthew 6:20 (GNT) — 20 Instead, store up riches for yourselves in heaven, where moths and rust cannot destroy, and robbers cannot break in and steal.*

[94]is stored. Understanding this, not as some distant reward, but rather as a current reality, changes the nature of how we live. The prophetic message of hope, "great is your reward in heaven", takes on different meaning, encouraging us to look at reward as more than just an eschatological hope. The trials and persecutions of this life then are cause for celebration. We will cheerfully face them full of joy because we know we already have our reward.

PROPHECY IS THE FRAMEWORK FOR LIFE

God intends then that we shape and order our life founded on his vision, giving us several streams and channels of guidance to lead us into our future destiny. The lack of understanding about this future destiny is often more a function of an unwillingness to listen or yield, rather than an omission by our Father in heaven. God is light, and therefore it is in his nature to bring future events to light. As his much-loved children, we can be confident he will reveal new things to us before they happen.[95]

> *John 16:13 (GNT) — 13 When, however, the Spirit comes, who reveals the truth about God, he will lead you into all the truth. He will not speak on his own authority, but he will speak of what he hears, and will tell you of things to come.*

"Prophetic insight guides into future truth."

---

[94] Matthew 5:12 (GNT) — 12 Be happy and glad, for a great reward is kept for you in heaven. This is how the prophets who lived before you were persecuted.; Luke 6:23 (GNT) — 23 Be glad when that happens, and dance for joy, because a great reward is kept for you in heaven. For their ancestors did the very same things to the prophets.

[95] Isaiah 42:9 (GNT) — 9 The things I predicted have now come true. Now I will tell you of new things even before they begin to happen."

For prophetic truth to be received, a change of lifestyle is imperative. Choices must be made which facilitate spending time with God and enable the individual to find their way into the presence of God. Someone must sit in the council of God or have received a visitation from God; this means finding the time.

When King Saul was given assurance through three detailed predictions, all fulfilled in that same day, Saul received affirmation through that fulfilment, which acknowledged him to be God's choice as king over Israel[96]. Yet such amazing and precisely fulfilled guidance does not necessarily result in an obedient lifestyle. Saul's experience of prophecy at his inauguration did not guarantee future compliance with the will of God in his life. Herein lies a warning, living today in the majestic presence of God is no guarantee that come tomorrow we will choose to do the same

And so prophetic truth comes as guidance, which must be heard or seen, received, understood, submitted to and enacted by faith.

For David, God's covenant word was dependable. God had spoken and in so doing, promised protection and victory against anyone who

---

[96] *1 Samuel 10:2–8 (GNT) — 2 when you leave me today, you will meet two men near Rachel's tomb at Zelzah in the territory of Benjamin. They will tell you that the donkeys you were looking for have been found, so that your father isn't worried any more about them but about you, and he keeps asking, 'What shall I do about my son?' 3 You will go on from there until you come to the sacred tree at Tabor, where you will meet three men on their way to offer a sacrifice to God at Bethel. One of them will be leading three young goats, another one will be carrying three loaves of bread, and the third one will have a leather bag full of wine. 4 They will greet you and offer you two of the loaves, which you are to accept. 5 Then you will go to the Hill of God in Gibeah, where there is a Philistine camp. At the entrance to the town you will meet a group of prophets coming down from the altar on the hill, playing harps, drums, flutes, and lyres. They will be dancing and shouting. 6 Suddenly the spirit of the LORD will take control of you, and you will join in their religious dancing and shouting and will become a different person. 7 When these things happen, do whatever God leads you to do. 8 You will go ahead of me to Gilgal, where I will meet you and offer burnt sacrifices and fellowship sacrifices. Wait there seven days until I come and tell you what to do."*

resists his intention to give the land to his people. This formed the basis of David's courage when he faced Goliath[97].

The personal experience of fulfilled covenantal promise emboldened David to seek the Lord in various campaigns.

> *1 Samuel 23:4–5 (GNT) — 4 So David consulted the LORD again, and the LORD said to him, "Go and attack Keilah, because I will give you victory over the Philistines." 5 So David and his men went to Keilah and attacked the Philistines; they killed many of them and took their livestock. And that was how David saved the town.*

The pursuit of the divine will was a key part of David's approach to life, from when he was a young man tending sheep. This attitude of first seeking the will of God became a key feature of how he governed the nation; he had a teachable spirit. His was not to be a lifestyle of presumption;[98] he would not act unless God had first spoken.

Prophecy in David's time was no secret pastime. Everyone around David knew about the prophetic intent of God for his life because Samuel had delivered a prophetic word from the Lord to him in front of his family. Later on, we find that even Jonathan, Saul's son, aligns[99]

---

[97] 1 Samuel 17:36–37 (GNT) — 36 I have killed lions and bears, and I will do the same to this heathen Philistine, who has defied the army of the living God. 37 The LORD has saved me from lions and bears; he will save me from this Philistine." "All right," Saul answered. "Go, and the LORD be with you."; 1 Samuel 17:46 (GNT) — 46 This very day the LORD will put you in my power; I will defeat you and cut off your head. And I will give the bodies of the Philistine soldiers to the birds and animals to eat. Then the whole world will know that Israel has a God,

Lessons. 1. he relied on a prophetic symbol of covenant relationship (circumcision). 2. He based his confidence on personal experience.

[98] The dangers of presumption

[99] 1 Samuel 23:17 (GNT) — 17 saying to him, "Don't be afraid. My father Saul won't be able to harm you. He knows very well that you are the one who will be the king of Israel and that I will be next in rank to you."

himself with David as a friend, in submission and with respect to God's prophetic will, accepting that David, rather than he, should succeed his father as king.

Despite Saul's expenditure of immense resources in an attempt to try and capture David and frustrate what he realised was God's plan, he failed. God, through repetition, again and again, has to teach man that once he has spoken to issue a decree, it is impossible to thwart that revealed divine will. At considerable cost to the nation, Saul embarked upon a vain vendetta to destroy David, a vanity which cost the nation its key military leadership and resulted in the loss of Saul's and Jonathan's lives[100] on the battlefield.

When one receives a prophetic word, it brings with it many encouragements, blessings or even warnings, which in the latter case can become a deterrent to sin. David found that being reminded about God's will for his life by Nabal's wife Abigail, he was kept from spilling blood in anger, thereby helping him to refrain from sin.[101] As in all things, future destiny is tied up with current obedience.

---

[100] *1 Samuel 24:2 (GNT) — 2 Saul took 3,000 of the best soldiers in Israel and went looking for David and his men east of Wild Goat Rocks.; 1 Samuel 26:2 (GNT) — 2 Saul went at once with 3,000 of the best soldiers in Israel to the wilderness of Ziph to look for David,*

[101] *1 Samuel 25:25–31 (GNT) — 25 Please, don't pay any attention to Nabal, that good-for-nothing! He is exactly what his name means—a fool! I wasn't there when your servants arrived, sir. 26 It is the LORD who has kept you from taking revenge and killing your enemies. And now I swear to you by the living LORD that your enemies and all who want to harm you will be punished like Nabal. 27 Please, sir, accept this present I have brought you, and give it to your men. 28 Please forgive me, sir, for any wrong I have done. The LORD will make you king, and your descendants also, because you are fighting his battles; and you will not do anything evil as long as you live. 29 If anyone should attack you and try to kill you, the LORD your God will keep you safe, as someone guards a precious treasure. As for your enemies, however, he will throw them away, as someone hurls stones with a sling. 30 And when the LORD has done all the good things he has promised you and has made you king of Israel, 31 then you will not have to feel regret or remorse, sir, for having killed without cause or for having taken your own revenge. And when the LORD has blessed you, sir, please do not forget me."*

For the twelve disciples the initial prophetic refrain "come follow me" was not only heard but instantly received. I often wonder if in those short encounters when Christ spoke, if he did so with the same kind of power that made the guards in the garden of Gethsemane fall at the sound of his voice.

> *"Engagement is the foundation for successful relationship."*

Peter Learned to Allow the Prophetic to Inspire his Life

Prophetic guidance led to success for Peter when he obeyed the instruction to let down his nets, which he did against his better judgment. Faith is different in nature to intellectual perception[102] or reasoning. His obedience led to a great catch of fish. This was a lesson which Peter would never forget.[103] Christ used prophetic instruction as part of his daily lifestyle, and he showed his disciples that the prophetic was to be exercised as part of normal daily living. He demonstrated that there are solutions to daily life to be accessed through prophetic inspiration. Paying his taxes was one such

---

[102] *Faith in relation to intellectual perception*

[103] *Luke 5:4–9 (GNT) — 4 When he finished speaking, he said to Simon, "Push the boat out further to the deep water, and you and your partners let down your nets for a catch." 5 "Master," Simon answered, "we worked hard all night long and caught nothing. But if you say so, I will let down the nets." 6 They let them down and caught such a large number of fish that the nets were about to break. 7 So they motioned to their partners in the other boat to come and help them. They came and filled both boats so full of fish that the boats were about to sink. 8 When Simon Peter saw what had happened, he fell on his knees before Jesus and said, "Go away from me, Lord! I am a sinful man!" 9 He and the others with him were all amazed at the large number of fish they had caught.*

Lessons. *1. To get a great catch don't overly lean on your experience. 2. If you know you have heard God take the risk.*

occasion[104] and finding a room for the last supper was another.[105] Prophetic revelation later brought Peter to the realisation that there was a way back after he had sinned. He was warned beforehand by Christ exactly how he would let the Lord down, a thought which was objectionable to him at the time.

"Redemptive history starts with a prophetic statement 'he will crush your heel'."

Jesus used this type of prophetic ministry to help Peter realise that although he would face the temptation to fall away from Christ,[106]

---

[104] *Matthew 17:27 (GNT) — 27 But we don't want to offend these people. So go to the lake and drop in a line. Pull up the first fish you hook, and in its mouth you will find a coin worth enough for my temple tax and yours. Take it and pay them our taxes."*

[105] *Mark 14:13–16 (GNT) — 13 Then Jesus sent two of them with these instructions: "Go into the city, and a man carrying a jar of water will meet you. Follow him 14 to the house he enters, and say to the owner of the house: 'The Teacher says, Where is the room where my disciples and I will eat the Passover meal?' 15 Then he will show you a large upstairs room, prepared and furnished, where you will get everything ready for us." 16 The disciples left, went to the city, and found everything just as Jesus had told them; and they prepared the Passover meal.*

[106] *Mark 14:30 (GNT) — 30 Jesus said to Peter, "I tell you that before the cock crows twice tonight, you will say three times that you do not know me." ; Mark 14:66–72 (GNT) — 66 Peter was still down in the courtyard when one of the High Priest's servant women came by. 67 When she saw Peter warming himself, she looked straight at him and said, "You, too, were with Jesus of Nazareth." 68 But he denied it. "I don't know ... I don't understand what you are talking about," he answered, and went out into the passage. Just then a cock crowed. 69 The servant woman saw him there and began to repeat to the bystanders, "He is one of them!" 70 But Peter denied it again. A little while later the bystanders accused Peter again, "You can't deny that you are one of them, because you, too, are from Galilee." 71 Then Peter said, "I swear that I am telling the truth! May God punish me if I am not! I do not know the man you are talking about!" 72 Just then a cock crowed a second time, and Peter remembered how Jesus had said to him, "Before the cock crows twice, you will say three times that you do not know me." And he broke down and cried.*

Peter would eventually repent of his denial.[107] A beautiful gesture which must have left him with a glimmer of hope, whilst the bitterness of his failure would have caused him many tears, for Peter loved Jesus with a passion.

"The prophetic believes in a profound and eternal sense of destiny"

Having eventually been restored by Christ, Peter would have had a profound sense of the destiny that awaited him. He had already been told that he would be foundational in the Genesis of the church[108], so when the day came to put on the mantle of leadership Peter was not found wanting. He was foundational in that 3,000 people were saved on the first day of Pentecost.[109]

---

[107] *Luke 22:32 (GNT) — 32 But I have prayed for you, Simon, that your faith will not fail. And when you turn back to me, you must strengthen your brothers."; John 21:15–17 (GNT) — 15 After they had eaten, Jesus said to Simon Peter, "Simon son of John, do you love me more than these others do?" "Yes, Lord," he answered, "you know that I love you." Jesus said to him, "Take care of my lambs." 16 A second time Jesus said to him, "Simon son of John, do you love me?" "Yes, Lord," he answered, "you know that I love you." Jesus said to him, "Take care of my sheep." 17 A third time Jesus said, "Simon son of John, do you love me?" Peter was sad because Jesus asked him the third time, "Do you love me?" so he said to him, "Lord, you know everything; you know that I love you!" Jesus said to him, "Take care of my sheep.*

[108] *Matthew 16:18 (GNT) — 18 And so I tell you, Peter: you are a rock, and on this rock foundation I will build my church, and not even death will ever be able to overcome it.*

[109] *Acts 1:15–16 (GNT) — 15 A few days later there was a meeting of the believers, about 120 in all, and Peter stood up to speak. 16 "My fellow-believers," he said, "the scripture had to come true in which the Holy Spirit, speaking through David, made a prediction about Judas, who was the guide for those who arrested Jesus.; Acts 2:14 (GNT) — 14 Then Peter stood up with the other eleven apostles and in a loud voice began to speak to the crowd: "Fellow-Jews and all of you who live in Jerusalem, listen to me and let me tell you what this means.; Acts 2:41 (GNT) — 41 Many of them believed his message and were baptized, and about 3,000 people were added to the group that day.*

He was foundational in that the first gentile believers were saved through his ministry.[110] Even this act of going to proclaim the gospel to the gentiles was prophetically received by Peter before the event itself.[111]

Again, this evangelistic as well as apostolic ministry, of both Peter and Andrew was prophesied by Christ at the beginning of their relationship with him. [112] Jesus was going to make them fishers of men. He was going to give them the skills they needed.

Describing such prophetic speaking as foretelling is important in this context. By foretelling future events, the Lord made known to Peter the difficulties he was going to encounter in obedience to God's purposes. Peter was told in separate, but explicit warnings, how he was going to die in the work of the Gospel. These warnings were

---

[110] *Acts 10:44–48 (GNT) — 44 While Peter was still speaking, the Holy Spirit came down on all those who were listening to his message. 45 The Jewish believers who had come from Joppa with Peter were amazed that God had poured out his gift of the Holy Spirit on the Gentiles also. 46 For they heard them speaking in strange tongues and praising God's greatness. Peter spoke up: 47 "These people have received the Holy Spirit, just as we also did. Can anyone, then, stop them from being baptized with water?" 48 So he ordered them to be baptized in the name of Jesus Christ. Then they asked him to stay with them for a few days.*

[111] *Acts 10:19–22 (GNT) — 19 Peter was still trying to understand what the vision meant, when the Spirit said, "Listen! Three men are here looking for you. 20 So get ready and go down, and do not hesitate to go with them, for I have sent them." 21 So Peter went down and said to the men, "I am the man you are looking for. Why have you come?" 22 "Captain Cornelius sent us," they answered. "He is a good man who worships God and is highly respected by all the Jewish people. An angel of God told him to invite you to his house, so that he could hear what you have to say."*

[112] *Mark 1:17 (GNT) — 17 Jesus said to them, "Come with me, and I will teach you to catch people."*

given to him shortly before he died.[113] We know from Tertullian in around 211 that Peter died by crucifixion during the Neronian Persecutions in 64AD.

How do we act at the point of receiving a prophetic message? Zechariah's response to what he heard demanded the immediate discipline of heaven; he was made dumb until the child promised to him was born. Zechariah's dumbness taught him that disbelief in the face of a clear prophetic voice could have painful consequences.[114] Nevertheless, judgement through prophetic utterance usually leaves us with some hope, because it is the communication of a loving Father to children he loves. The story of Hezekiah gives us an example of this. Having initially been judged by God and condemned to death, God, in hearing his sobs and seeing his tears, relented. He confirmed his change of heart to Hezekiah through the backward travelling of the shadow on the steps of his palace, to show by a miracle that Hezekiah's life had been spared. God can relent when he gives a

---

[113] *John 13:36–37 (GNT) — 36 "Where are you going, Lord?" Simon Peter asked him. "You cannot follow me now where I am going," answered Jesus; "but later you will follow me." 37 "Lord, why can't I follow you now?" asked Peter. "I am ready to die for you!"; 2 Peter 1:13–16 (GNT) — 13 I think it only right for me to stir up your memory of these matters as long as I am still alive. 14 I know that I shall soon put off this mortal body, as our Lord Jesus Christ plainly told me. 15 I will do my best, then, to provide a way for you to remember these matters at all times after my death. 16 We have not depended on made-up stories in making known to you the mighty coming of our Lord Jesus Christ. With our own eyes we saw his greatness.;*

[114] *Luke 1:13 (GNT) — 13 But the angel said to him, "Don't be afraid, Zechariah! God has heard your prayer, and your wife Elizabeth will bear you a son. You are to name him John. ; Luke 1:20–22 (GNT) — 20 But you have not believed my message, which will come true at the right time. Because you have not believed, you will be unable to speak; you will remain silent until the day my promise to you comes true." 21 In the meantime the people were waiting for Zechariah and wondering why he was spending such a long time in the Temple. 22 When he came out, he could not speak to them, and so they knew that he had seen a vision in the Temple. Unable to say a word, he made signs to them with his hands.*

strong, challenging prophetic word showing that even in judgement he will show mercy.[115]

INSPIRATION GIVES BIRTH TO HEROES

Hebrews 11:30–32 (GNT) — 30 It was faith that made the walls of Jericho fall down after the Israelites had marched round them for seven days. 31 It was faith that kept the prostitute Rahab from being killed with those who disobeyed God, for she gave the Israelite spies a friendly welcome. 32 Should I go on? There isn't enough time for me to speak of Gideon, Barak, Samson, Jephthah, David, Samuel, and the prophets.

Why was a woman like Rahab included in the list of amazing heroes in Hebrews chapter 11? From the Old Testament, we know she was a prostitute.[116] She was someone who brazenly sold herself for money.[117] Clearly, her previous life and character was not why she

---

[115] 2 Kings 20:1–12 (GNT) — 1 About this time King Hezekiah fell ill and almost died. The prophet Isaiah son of Amoz went to see him and said to him, "The LORD tells you that you are to put everything in order, because you will not recover. Get ready to die." 2 Hezekiah turned his face to the wall and prayed: 3 "Remember, LORD, that I have served you faithfully and loyally, and that I have always tried to do what you wanted me to." And he began to cry bitterly. 4 Isaiah left the king, but before he had passed through the central courtyard of the palace the LORD told him 5 to go back to Hezekiah, ruler of the LORD's people, and say to him, "I, the LORD, the God of your ancestor David, have heard your prayer and seen your tears. I will heal you, and in three days you will go to the Temple. 6 I will let you live fifteen years longer. I will rescue you and this city of Jerusalem from the emperor of Assyria. I will defend this city, for the sake of my own honour and because of the promise I made to my servant David." 7 Then Isaiah told the king's attendants to put on his boil a paste made of figs, and he would get well. 8 King Hezekiah asked, "What is the sign to prove that the LORD will heal me and that three days later I will be able to go to the Temple?" 9 Isaiah replied, "The LORD will give you a sign to prove that he will keep his promise. Now, would you prefer the shadow on the stairway to go forward ten steps or go back ten steps?" 10 Hezekiah answered, "It's easy to make the shadow go forward ten steps! Make it go back ten steps." 11 Isaiah prayed to the LORD, and the LORD made the shadow go back ten steps on the stairway set up by King Ahaz. 12 About that same time the king of Babylonia, Merodach Baladan, the son of Baladan, heard that King Hezekiah had been ill, so he sent him a letter and a present.

[116] Joshua 2:1-7

[117] Jeremiah 3:3

was included in Hebrews 11. Before we lose ourselves in an outrage of moralising, it is good to remember that prostitution is not limited to those who sell their body for sex. There are many ways that people prostitute themselves.[118]

People sell themselves for secret information that empowers, as promised by false religions. They sell themselves for news from the dead through participation in things like séances. People sell themselves for security to a job, doing things which offend their conscience. People sell themselves for popularity. People who corrupt themselves in such ways will at some point suffer for their indiscretions.[119] Allowing the human conscience to be violated by selling one's principles in order to gain something, is prostitution.

Very often those who end up prostituting themselves need never to have done so. Rahab could probably have married any man she wanted, for according to rabbinical tradition, Rahab was one of the four most beautiful women in the world. So, what is there to consider about Rahab? Why was she included in the Hebrews hall of fame?

She was commended for two things. First, she was commended because she chose to turn her back on a way of life that was wicked. She recognised that whatever powers existed, whatever security the walls provided, whatever protection she was offered by the armies in

---

[118] *Leviticus 20:6 (GNT) — 6 "If anyone goes for advice to people who consult the spirits of the dead, I will turn against him and will no longer consider him one of my people.*

[119] *Revelation 19:2 (GNT) — 2 True and just are his judgements! He has condemned the prostitute who was corrupting the earth with her immorality. God has punished her because she killed his servants."*

the city, <u>she knew</u> that it was better to trust in God.[120] She aligned her hopes for her future prosperity to what she understood as the revealed will of God.

She moved from fear to faith[121], from simply believing in God to following him, from opposition to God, to acceptance of God, and from enmity towards God, to becoming a friend of God.

God told his people that the city was going to be theirs and she, like the people of God, aligned her faith with their faith and believed him.[122] She also was spoken well of in scripture because she was charitable; hiding the spies who had come into the city and thus saving their lives.[123] Her actions on that fateful day led to her becoming accepted by the people of God at the time. Later on, we find she became the wife of Salmon. Their son Boaz married Ruth and became the father of Obed, the grandfather of Jesse, and the great-grandfather of David. Thus, a Canaanite prostitute became part of the

---

[120] *Joshua 2:8–12 (GNT)* — *8 Before the spies settled down for the night, Rahab went up on the roof 9 and said to them, "I know that the LORD has given you this land. Everyone in the country is terrified of you. 10 We have heard how the LORD dried up the Red Sea in front of you when you were leaving Egypt. We have also heard how you killed Sihon and Og, the two Amorite kings east of the Jordan. 11 We were afraid as soon as we heard about it; we have all lost our courage because of you. The LORD your God is God in heaven above and here on earth. 12 Now swear by him that you will treat my family as kindly as I have treated you, and give me some sign that I can trust you.*

[121] <u>Fear and Faith</u> *Fear reveals a lack of trust in God*

[122] *Joshua 6:16 (GNT)* — *16 The seventh time round, when the priests were about to sound the trumpets, Joshua ordered the people to shout, and he said, "The LORD has given you the city!*

[123] *James 2:25 (GNT)* — *25 It was the same with the prostitute Rahab. She was put right with God through her actions, by welcoming the Israelite spies and helping them to escape by a different road.*

lineage of King David out of which the Messiah came.[124] A prostitute became a descendant of Jesus Christ himself.

An interesting theological question is buried deep within this account. How could she be included in the genealogy of Jesus, when in the process of saving the spies she lied? Is this an advert for ungodliness as a means to helping God? Is a little lie okay as long as it is for a right cause? Does God accept wickedness in a good cause? The Bible never teaches that sin in the cause of averting a greater evil is ever acceptable.[125]

It is a contradiction for a Christian to rely solely on the grace of God as a basis for doing what he likes. God demands that we all die to our old life.[126] God hates lies in any case.[127] Jesus is the way, the truth and the life and therefore cannot be party to falsehoods.

Rahab is a prophetic picture of Christ accepting fallen humanity. In the desire to do good we do many things which offend God, yet he

---

[124] *Matthew 1:5 V*

[125] *Romans 3:8–9 (GNT) — 8 Why not say, then, "Let us do evil so that good may come"? Some people, indeed, have insulted me by accusing me of saying this very thing! They will be condemned, as they should be. 9 Well then, are we Jews in any better condition than the Gentiles? Not at all! I have already shown that Jews and Gentiles alike are all under the power of sin.*

[126] *Romans 6:1–5 (GNT) — 1 What shall we say, then? Should we continue to live in sin so that God's grace will increase? 2 Certainly not! We have died to sin—how then can we go on living in it? 3 For surely you know that when we were baptized into union with Christ Jesus, we were baptized into union with his death. 4 By our baptism, then, we were buried with him and shared his death, in order that, just as Christ was raised from death by the glorious power of the Father, so also we might live a new life. 5 For since we have become one with him in dying as he did, in the same way we shall be one with him by being raised to life as he was.*

[127] *Hebrews 6:18 (GNT) — 18 There are these two things, then, that cannot change and about which God cannot lie. So we who have found safety with him are greatly encouraged to hold firmly to the hope placed before us.; 1 John 1:6 (GNT) — 6 If, then, we say that we have fellowship with him, yet at the same time live in the darkness, we are lying both in our words and in our actions.*

accepts us still. If God can, through grace, save the most wicked of people and make them family, then there is hope for us all, because acceptance into God's family is a function of God's grace and not our works.[128]

---

[128] *Matthew 21:31 (GNT) — 31 Which one of the two did what his father wanted?" "The elder one," they answered. So Jesus said to them, "I tell you: the tax collectors and the prostitutes are going into the Kingdom of God ahead of you.*

Understanding Prophecy

IS EVERY PROPHECY CLEAR?

Did Old Testament Prophets Understand Their Prophecies?

Old Testament prophet's prophesied with pinpoint accuracy. There was no lack of detail or precision with the revelations they discharged. They received prophecies much in the same way modern dictation machines operate today.

They simply repeated what they heard. Of course, they received the prophecies through mechanisms such as dreams and visions; traditional means familiar with those who receive such prophecies today. The biggest difference between them and us is that their function was not as sons and daughters, with all the attendant difficulties, relational and educational, that accompany the relationship between a father and his children. No, Old Testament prophets functioned more like mechanical recorders in the delivery of what they heard.

Their New Testament counterparts, on the other hand, are individuals who are in the process of being transformed into the image of Christ. As works in the process of being transformed by the Father, they can only regurgitate the prophetic revelations which they have both seen and heard in part. Because of this, the Old Testament prophets demonstrated a greater accuracy than we currently experience.

Nevertheless, like us, Israel's prophets were keen to have insight into the meaning of what they were seeing and saying. They searched diligently, trying to understand their own predictions.[129] Even though Daniel was seen as a great administrative prophet, he sometimes confessed ignorance as to the meaning of his own predictions. But this did not in any way indicate that there was any inaccuracy in what he was seeing, just a lack of understanding of its meaning.[130]

Some Old Testament figures even spoke prophetically without understanding at the time that they were speaking prophetically.[131] God will use any prophetic vehicle, or life moment, within which to release prophetic insight that he cares to. And so, Abraham, leading his son Isaac up the mountain as an offering unto the Lord, speaks out, stating that the Lord will provide an offering, only later on realising that he was speaking prophetically. Similarly, we see the high

---

[129] *1 Peter 1:10–11 (NRSV) — 10 Concerning this salvation, the prophets who prophesied of the grace that was to be yours made careful search and inquiry, 11 inquiring about the person or time that the Spirit of Christ within them indicated when it testified in advance to the sufferings destined for Christ and the subsequent glory.*

[130] *Daniel 8:27 (NRSV) — 27 So I, Daniel, was overcome and lay sick for some days; then I arose and went about the king's business. But I was dismayed by the vision and did not understand it.; Zechariah 4:13 (NRSV) — 13 He said to me, "Do you not know what these are?" I said, "No, my lord."; Daniel 12:8 (NRSV) — 8 I heard but could not understand; so I said, "My lord, what shall be the outcome of these things?"*

[131] *Genesis 22:7–8 (NRSV) — 7 Isaac said to his father Abraham, "Father!" And he said, "Here I am, my son." He said, "The fire and the wood are here, but where is the lamb for a burnt offering?" 8 Abraham said, "God himself will provide the lamb for a burnt offering, my son." So the two of them walked on together.*

priest Caiaphas prophesying over Jesus without realising he was speaking prophetically.[132]

When is Prophecy Literal?

Most prophecies of scripture are spoken as a literally expressed declaration. They refer to events that are about to, or which have already taken place.[133] In general, prophecies should not be dismissed as non-literal unless; the context is clearly symbolic or to speak of it in a literal manner would make what was said completely incomprehensible and bizarre, or the prophecy itself makes clear it is not literal. It is important to carefully note the context of the prophecy and divine intent contained in it. So, with study, we come to understand that "the virgin will be with child" (Isaiah 7:14), whilst literally applying to King Ahaz's time also had a secondary application foretelling the coming of Christ.

THE RICHNESS OF PROPHETIC LANGUAGE

Prophetic language is rich and not limited to one type of creative expression. The variety of approach reflecting the beauty God sees in

---

[132] *John 11:49–52 (NRSV) — 49 But one of them, Caiaphas, who was high priest that year, said to them, "You know nothing at all! 50 You do not understand that it is better for you to have one man die for the people than to have the whole nation destroyed." 51 He did not say this on his own, but being high priest that year he prophesied that Jesus was about to die for the nation, 52 and not for the nation only, but to gather into one the dispersed children of God.*

[133] *Exodus 7:15–17 (NRSV) — 15 Go to Pharaoh in the morning, as he is going out to the water; stand by at the river bank to meet him, and take in your hand the staff that was turned into a snake. 16 Say to him, 'The LORD, the God of the Hebrews, sent me to you to say, "Let my people go, so that they may worship me in the wilderness." But until now you have not listened. 17 Thus says the LORD, "By this you shall know that I am the LORD." See, with the staff that is in my hand I will strike the water that is in the Nile, and it shall be turned to blood.*

diversity. Not only is the language used diverse, the methods by which God communicates are also diverse.

God uses poetic language to touch the soul and the imagination of the individual. He uses this sort of language as a doorway into a believer's heart, our faith being reflected in our feelings. Other literary tools are employed, such as metaphors, to give a non-literal comparison of one thing with another, or an allegory, which is a story with deep meaning, or truth being symbolically expressed. Types of narrative include; prophetic song, poetic prophecy, representative prophecy, in which one thing represents a truth, person or object; comparative prophecy in which the behaviour, or a person, or an object is compared to others; descriptive poetry or dramatised prophecy, in which the prophet's message is enacted or dramatised in a public way.

Examples of such poetic usage are found throughout scripture.[134] Esau and Jacob are figuratively speaking, two nations in Rebekah's womb.[135] Psalm 23 is an amazing combination of metaphors to convey truth, as is the picture of the lampstand in the Book of Revelation. At other times visual aids[136] are sometimes used to get

---

[134] *metaphors, allegory prophetic song, poetic prophecy, Representative prophecy, Comparative prophecy, dramatised prophecy.*

[135] *Genesis 25:23 (NRSV) — 23 And the LORD said to her, "Two nations are in your womb, and two peoples born of you shall be divided; the one shall be stronger than the other, the elder shall serve the younger."*

[136] *Jeremiah 13:1 (NRSV) — 1 Thus said the LORD to me, "Go and buy yourself a linen loincloth, and put it on your loins, but do not dip it in water."; Jeremiah 19:1 (NRSV) — 1 Thus said the LORD: Go and buy a potter's earthenware jug. Take with you some of the elders of the people and some of the senior priests,; Jeremiah 28:10 (NRSV) — 10 Then the prophet Hananiah took the yoke from the neck of the prophet Jeremiah, and broke it. ; Jeremiah 43:9 (NRSV) — 9 Take some large stones in your hands and bury them in the clay pavement that is at the entrance to Pharaoh's palace in Tahpanhes. Let the Judeans see you do it,*

across the point of the message. Ezekiel and Jeremiah used these to great effect to convey their message.

Prophetic Symbols as Teaching Aids

The scriptures employ the use of prophetic symbols as teaching aids. These symbols can be described as a "type". A type is the use of a pattern as a means of comparing an expected future event, with a current one. Types are prophetic in nature.[137] In the New Testament 'type' conveys a wide range of meaning and is translated as such, for example; a type could be a mark [138] or a pattern[139]. A type is meant, in the words of the Apostle Paul, to be an example worthy of note and consideration, as demonstrated in the example of his life as a pattern those who also ministered, ought to follow.[140] In prophetic usage, a type is a significant symbol which has at least two meanings; firstly the literal thing or event spoken of, and secondly a deeper truth of which that type is being spoken of, stands for. For example, the

---

[137] *in the greek " tupos" is a figure, form, manner, pattern, print.*

[138] *John 20:25 (NRSV) — 25 So the other disciples told him, "We have seen the Lord." But he said to them, "Unless I see the mark of the nails in his hands, and put my finger in the mark of the nails and my hand in his side, I will not believe."*

[139] *Acts 7:44 (NRSV) — 44 "Our ancestors had the tent of testimony in the wilderness, as God directed when he spoke to Moses, ordering him to make it according to the pattern he had seen.; Romans 5:14 (NRSV) — 14 Yet death exercised dominion from Adam to Moses, even over those whose sins were not like the transgression of Adam, who is a type of the one who was to come.*

[140] *2 Thessalonians 3:9 (NRSV) — 9 This was not because we do not have that right, but in order to give you an example to imitate.*

tabernacle built by Moses also stands for the heavenly type of which the earthly is but a copy.[141]

A type may speak of a specific act of the Lord.[142] God uses a wide variety of things as types. Types can be people like Adam, or they can be events such as crossing the Red Sea. Types can be objects such as the temple or, institutions such as the Sabbath. It can stand for that which makes you clean, as in the ceremonial release of the scapegoat.

A type then had a dual purpose. It stands for something current, which the hearer to some extent understands; but it also corresponds to a future event or thing which it is a type of, or which it symbolically represents. So previous covenants were a "type" of the new covenant in Christ.[143] The millions of sacrifices made in the Old Testament worship of Yahweh were a pointer to the sacrifice of Christ on the Cross.[144] Types were images casting their metaphoric shadow from a point remote in the future, through time itself, into our current

---

[141] *Hebrews 8:5–6 (NRSV) — 5 They offer worship in a sanctuary that is a sketch and shadow of the heavenly one; for Moses, when he was about to erect the tent, was warned, "See that you make everything according to the pattern that was shown you on the mountain." 6 But Jesus has now obtained a more excellent ministry, and to that degree he is the mediator of a better covenant, which has been enacted through better promises.*

[142] *Numbers 21:9 (NRSV) — 9 So Moses made a serpent of bronze, and put it upon a pole; and whenever a serpent bit someone, that person would look at the serpent of bronze and live. ; John 3:14 (NRSV) — 14 And just as Moses lifted up the serpent in the wilderness, so must the Son of Man be lifted up,*

[143] *Hebrews 9:15 (NRSV) — 15 For this reason he is the mediator of a new covenant, so that those who are called may receive the promised eternal inheritance, because a death has occurred that redeems them from the transgressions under the first covenant.; Hebrews 11:40 (NRSV) — 40 since God had provided something better so that they would not, apart from us, be made perfect.*

[144] *Hebrews 9:9–10 (NRSV) — 9 This is a symbol of the present time, during which gifts and sacrifices are offered that cannot perfect the conscience of the worshiper, 10 but deal only with food and drink and various baptisms, regulations for the body imposed until the time comes to set things right.*

history and behind us deep into the past.[145] This has implications for the meaning behind the feasts and ceremonies. For example, the Feast of Tabernacles is a foreshadow of the ingathering of nations.[146]

Sometimes a prophetic symbolic type unveils an immense amount of future revelation, granting the hearer a great deal of knowledge. Such are some of the prophecies, for example, which relate to the trials of Jesus Christ as he endured the cross. The Passover lamb was not to have any of its bones broken, a type of Christ being spared that indignity on the cross.[147] The sin offering,[148] another type which relates to Christ, was to be burned outside the camp. Again, Christ was taken outside the city gate to be crucified.

Scripture Explains Prophetic Symbols

Scripture often interprets these prophetic symbols in order that we might understand them; each of these prophetic symbols standing for spiritual realities, as well as literal ones. When a symbolic name is given in the prophecy, it can sometimes explain what is intended. A tree of life is scriptures earliest and probably widest known symbol

---

[145] Hebrews 10:1 (NRSV) — 1 Since the law has only a shadow of the good things to come and not the true form of these realities, it can never, by the same sacrifices that are continually offered year after year, make perfect those who approach.

[146] Zechariah 14:16 (NRSV) — 16 Then all who survive of the nations that have come against Jerusalem shall go up year after year to worship the King, the LORD of hosts, and to keep the festival of booths.

[147] Exodus 12:46 (NRSV) — 46 It shall be eaten in one house; you shall not take any of the animal outside the house, and you shall not break any of its bones.; John 19:35–36 (NRSV) — 35 (He who saw this has testified so that you also may believe. His testimony is true, and he knows that he tells the truth.) 36 These things occurred so that the scripture might be fulfilled, "None of his bones shall be broken."

[148] Leviticus 4:12 (NRSV) — 12 all the rest of the bull—he shall carry out to a clean place outside the camp, to the ash heap, and shall burn it on a wood fire; at the ash heap it shall be burned. ; Hebrews 13:12 (NRSV) — 12 Therefore Jesus also suffered outside the city gate in order to sanctify the people by his own blood.

outside the context of Church; the name speaks for itself.[149] In his revelation to Amos, the Lord uses the symbol of a basket of ripe fruit as a depiction of the season of his judgement[150] over Israel; again the name 'basket of ripe fruit' speaks for itself and explains what is intended by the prophecy.

The context of the prophecy can also explain the prophetic symbol being used.[151] When Joseph saw the sheaves of wheat bowing down to his sheaf, his brothers were not ignorant of the implication, and they knew exactly what was meant by the prophetic symbolism and what was being suggested about the future direction of their relationship with him.[152]

---

[149] *Genesis 2:9 (NRSV) — 9 Out of the ground the LORD God made to grow every tree that is pleasant to the sight and good for food, the tree of life also in the midst of the garden, and the tree of the knowledge of good and evil.*

[150] *Amos 8:1–3 (NRSV) — 1 This is what the Lord GOD showed me—a basket of summer fruit. 2 He said, "Amos, what do you see?" And I said, "A basket of summer fruit." Then the LORD said to me, "The end has come upon my people Israel; I will never again pass them by. 3 The songs of the temple shall become wailings in that day," says the Lord GOD; "the dead bodies shall be many, cast out in every place. Be silent!"*

[151] *Zechariah 3:8–10 (NRSV) — 8 Now listen, Joshua, high priest, you and your colleagues who sit before you! For they are an omen of things to come: I am going to bring my servant the Branch. 9 For on the stone that I have set before Joshua, on a single stone with seven facets, I will engrave its inscription, says the LORD of hosts, and I will remove the guilt of this land in a single day. 10 On that day, says the LORD of hosts, you shall invite each other to come under your vine and fig tree."; Zechariah 4:8–10 (NRSV) — 8 Moreover the word of the LORD came to me, saying, 9 "The hands of Zerubbabel have laid the foundation of this house; his hands shall also complete it. Then you will know that the LORD of hosts has sent me to you. 10 For whoever has despised the day of small things shall rejoice, and shall see the plummet in the hand of Zerubbabel. "These seven are the eyes of the LORD, which range through the whole earth."*

[152] *Genesis 37:7–8 (NRSV) — 7 There we were, binding sheaves in the field. Suddenly my sheaf rose and stood upright; then your sheaves gathered around it, and bowed down to my sheaf." 8 His brothers said to him, "Are you indeed to reign over us? Are you indeed to have dominion over us?" So they hated him even more because of his dreams and his words.*

Is all Prophecy Inescapable?

All of God's will is inescapable.[153] There is a clear sense in which this is already revealed; history culminates in a new heaven and earth. But it is also true that some prophecy carries a conditional "if", indicating that a response is required for the prophecy to be activated or enacted. Then there are prophecies which imply that God is providing a reward but requires the recipient to perform some action in order to receive the prophetic promise, such as God promising the land to his people as a gift. Despite the gift, it was required that his people had to fight for the land given to them.

The call I received to plant churches with my wife Fiona was conditional. We suffered a great setback with the first church plant that challenged our joy, zeal, enthusiasm and call. But despite it, we held on to the prophetic word that had been received, and now we thank God that we did. Others in the face of opposition have given up and in so doing have missed their prophetic vocation. Yet even if we do fail to respond at first adequately, there is always hope. God is kind and merciful, and even if we do get it wrong, our Father in heaven is kind, as demonstrated in the story of Hezekiah, which we

---

[153] *1 Kings 13:1-22*

looked at previously. Repentance can at times change the prophetic fortunes of those who had previously been disobedient.[154]

Discerning the spirit behind a prophecy is therefore of paramount importance. It is vital to determine whether it is the Spirit of the Lord or another spirit at work. A lack of discernment would, at best, mean submitting your life to another's mistaken vision for your life; at worst it would mean following the will of the demonic forces.

The character of the prophet is as important as the message the prophet brings. If the character does not fit, it could be an indication that the prophetic message itself is false. Humility is an essential character trait of a prophet, Moses the greatest prophet of all was also the most humble.

The Key to Interpreting Prophecy

Scripture is our prophetically inspired legacy.[155] Scripture as the spoken word[156] of God is authoritative in all matters of interpretation, carrying with it unlimited inspirational power because it comes by

---

[154] *2 Kings 20:1–6 (NRSV) — 1 In those days Hezekiah became sick and was at the point of death. The prophet Isaiah son of Amoz came to him, and said to him, "Thus says the LORD: Set your house in order, for you shall die; you shall not recover." 2 Then Hezekiah turned his face to the wall and prayed to the LORD: 3 "Remember now, O LORD, I implore you, how I have walked before you in faithfulness with a whole heart, and have done what is good in your sight." Hezekiah wept bitterly. 4 Before Isaiah had gone out of the middle court, the word of the LORD came to him: 5 "Turn back, and say to Hezekiah prince of my people, Thus says the LORD, the God of your ancestor David: I have heard your prayer, I have seen your tears; indeed, I will heal you; on the third day you shall go up to the house of the LORD. 6 I will add fifteen years to your life. I will deliver you and this city out of the hand of the king of Assyria; I will defend this city for my own sake and for my servant David's sake."*

[155] *Inspirational facts about scripture include...*

[156] *Isaiah 34:16 (NRSV) — 16 Seek and read from the book of the LORD: Not one of these shall be missing; none shall be without its mate. For the mouth of the LORD has commanded, and his spirit has gathered them.*

means of the Holy Spirit.[157] Of course, some live in the realm of debating the meaning, content, and even the source of scripture. The true believer receives, meditates on, and believes the word of God.

Indifference to God's written word is not something that pleases God.[158] Given the weight of evidence concerning fulfilled prophecy, it is foolishness not to believe what the prophets have written.[159] To consider them to be stories, or simply as something that contains the word of God, demands the individual to willfully ignore examples of fulfilled prophecy contained in scripture, which are too numerous for the pages of this book.

The Emmaus Road experience is typical of how written prophetic revelations are often experienced. It starts with disappointed disciples walking on the Emmaus Road heading home and ends up with them excited and inspired at their experience and revelation of the risen Christ. With such occurrences, scripture is "opened" up to us, and when it is, the effect it has is to cause our hearts to almost literally burn in our chest.

> *Luke 24:32 (NRSV) — 32 They said to each other, "Were not our hearts burning within us while he was talking to us on the road, while he was opening the scriptures to us?"*

---

[157] 2 Peter 1:20–21 (NRSV) — 20 First of all you must understand this, that no prophecy of scripture is a matter of one's own interpretation, 21 because no prophecy ever came by human will, but men and women moved by the Holy Spirit spoke from God.

[158] Zechariah 7:12 (NRSV) — 12 They made their hearts adamant in order not to hear the law and the words that the LORD of hosts had sent by his spirit through the former prophets. Therefore great wrath came from the LORD of hosts.

[159] Luke 24:25–27 (NRSV) — 25 Then he said to them, "Oh, how foolish you are, and how slow of heart to believe all that the prophets have declared! 26 Was it not necessary that the Messiah should suffer these things and then enter into his glory?" 27 Then beginning with Moses and all the prophets, he interpreted to them the things about himself in all the scriptures.

The Seduction of False Seers

The advantage of being able to see beyond the natural was not lost on kings or ordinary people. The advantage in warfare is obvious; intelligence is a key to victory in any battle and the prophetic ability to see, grants a competitive advantage. With such an advantage it becomes possible to plan an effective military strategy in order to win the battle. Hitler reportedly had occult influences which affected and influenced him in his quest for power, and we know that other national leaders, like Roosevelt, toyed with occultism. This invitation to know more is what the serpent promised Adam and Eve; their eyes would 'be opened' if they ate of the fruit of the tree of knowledge of good and evil. Interestingly the Hebrew word for eye is singular. Here Satan promises increased knowledge and understanding, the same bait he has used to ensnare people over the ages. If people serve Satan, he promises them insight, revelation and understanding and so you will find the symbol of the eye at the heart of many occult traditions. He still promises the same things centuries later.

Greed provided many opportunities for unscrupulous fraudsters to claim they were seers sent by God.[160] However, God reserves

---

[160] *Deuteronomy 13:1–5 (NRSV) — 1 If prophets or those who divine by dreams appear among you and promise you omens or portents, 2 and the omens or the portents declared by them take place, and they say, "Let us follow other gods" (whom you have not known) "and let us serve them," 3 you must not heed the words of those prophets or those who divine by dreams; for the LORD your God is testing you, to know whether you indeed love the LORD your God with all your heart and soul. 4 The LORD your God you shall follow, him alone you shall fear, his commandments you shall keep, his voice you shall obey, him you shall serve, and to him you shall hold fast. 5 But those prophets or those who divine by dreams shall be put to death for having spoken treason against the LORD your God—who brought you out of the land of Egypt and redeemed you from the house of slavery—to turn you from the way in which the LORD your God commanded you to walk. So you shall purge the evil from your midst.*

judgement for all false prophets.[161] This battle does not just have a human face; there are also demonic elements, fallen spirits which war against mankind in order to further lead them away from God.[162]

The imperative requirement to judge prophecy, applies as much to those outside the family of God as to those inside it. For claimed prophetic insight can have only one of three sources; God, Satan, or the human mind.

---

[161] *Jeremiah 23:27–32 (NRSV) — 27 They plan to make my people forget my name by their dreams that they tell one another, just as their ancestors forgot my name for Baal. 28 Let the prophet who has a dream tell the dream, but let the one who has my word speak my word faithfully. What has straw in common with wheat? says the LORD. 29 Is not my word like fire, says the LORD, and like a hammer that breaks a rock in pieces? 30 See, therefore, I am against the prophets, says the LORD, who steal my words from one another. 31 See, I am against the prophets, says the LORD, who use their own tongues and say, "Says the LORD." 32 See, I am against those who prophesy lying dreams, says the LORD, and who tell them, and who lead my people astray by their lies and their recklessness, when I did not send them or appoint them; so they do not profit this people at all, says the LORD.*

[162] *1 Samuel 18:10 (NRSV) — 10 The next day an evil spirit from God rushed upon Saul, and he raved within his house, while David was playing the lyre, as he did day by day. Saul had his spear in his hand;*

The Habitation of a Prophet

The True Meaning of the Keys to Father's House

Because the prophet is an intimate son or daughter of the Father and as such, a trusted child, they carry in their possession Father's house keys. The moment a child comes of age, parents agonise over whether they should be given keys to the house. Our heavenly Father deems us ready.

Out of relationship with the Father, he gives us keys of the kingdom, but these have often been misunderstood. They are in fact a prophetic instrument, a point I will explain in a moment. Firstly, it is worth noting that they are relational keys, granted purely by virtue of the fact that the believer is in a relationship with God and a disciple of Jesus Christ. The mature child of God chooses to live in receipt of the responsibility to steward these keys, which have the ability to unlock circumstances and open doors. Demonstrating a lifestyle reflective of the Father by properly utilising keys of the kingdom.[163] This prophetic

---

[163] *Matthew 16:17–20 (NKJV)* — *17 Jesus answered and said to him, "Blessed are you, Simon Bar-Jonah, for flesh and blood has not revealed this to you, but My Father who is in heaven. 18 And I also say to you that you are Peter, and on this rock I will build My church, and the gates of Hades shall not prevail against it. 19 And I will give you the keys of the kingdom of heaven, and whatever you bind on earth will be bound in heaven, and whatever you loose on earth will be loosed in heaven." 20 Then He commanded His disciples that they should tell no one that He was Jesus the Christ.*

ability and responsibility to bind and loose is given to all the disciples and not just to Peter.[164]

Peter's discovery of who Christ is prompts Jesus to reveal his chief purpose; "I will build my church", a temple built not by human hands,[165] but rather a spiritual house[166] built for God. God is not just interested in seating us with him in heavenly places; he is determined to live with us in earthly ones. This is why any definition of the church will be contested. There will be those who seek to demote the church, to exclude any form of authoritative or structural strength, not always understanding that they are resisting divine will.

Yet the kingdom must continue to advance because Jesus is building his church. He is not building his kingdom; he is building his church. We cannot extend his kingdom, for there is no realm in which he is not King of Kings and Lord of Lords. We can lay hold of this kingdom, enter it, be ruled by it and reflect it in our works, because the kingdom is within us. But our works are not the kingdom, because the kingdom is the rule and reign of Christ within us. The kingdom is advancing because Jesus is enforcing his governance, the increase of which there will be no end in human hearts, and all of creation will submit to that rule. This kingdom is given to him by the Father, but his mission is the building up of the church. Consequently, church is the chief battleground, the edifice Satan and those who unwittingly taken in by him seek, to deconstruct.

The prophet mainly speaks to this challenge. The religious spirit steers toward building organisations and institutions. The Christian, living in

---

[164] *Mat 18:18*

[165] *1 Cor 3:11-16*

[166] *1 Pet 2:5*

the spirit, seeks to build up believers into committed communities, enabling them to become effective tools in the hands of Christ. The former is back to front, the latter the right way up. This is a matter of priority. Institutions external to the church will be impacted by radical Christians coming out of these committed communities, but they are never to be a substitute for the church. Institutions measure performance by how much you achieve; genuine Christian relationships measure performance by how much you love.

Applying the Keys? What does it Mean?

Applying the keys means having the authority to act, but in what sense? Jesus builds on rabbinic language but elevates the concept to a higher level. In traditional rabbinic language; binding meant to forbid, making religious law tighter, and loosing meant to make religious laws slacker, or permitting behaviour. When Jesus uses this language, he is saying something very different. When Jesus uses the language of binding and loosing, he is saying that whatever you bind on earth will have already been bound in heaven. Having listened to what heaven has to say, the prophet uses analogies and prophetic symbolism to deliver heavenly instruction, using them as keys to unlock doors and to apply the authority of heaven.

Remember that Jesus did not do anything that he did not see his Father doing, nor say anything he did not hear his Father saying; relational intimacy, resulting in relational integrity. What he is saying, is that because we stand before the Father, we are able to see and hear, and therefore share with others, what the Father is saying, with heaven backing it up. Because we stand before the throne of God, we can explain his prophetic will.

Prayer then for the prophet, becomes an overflow of what God is already doing as witnessed in the courts of heaven, because just like Elisha, the prophet sees what God is decreeing in heaven. It forms the backbone of the prophet's prayer life. The authority of the keys is realised and activated through relationship; it is not just the judicial transaction of the cross. Nor is it the unified agreement of a group of believers, but rather a prophetic function. There are keys which only Christ commands;[167] and then there are those keys which are freely available to sons and daughters, who in honour, enter the courts of heaven.

This Present Power

The prophet of God commands the experience of an open heaven, meaning they bring the experience of heaven to bear. This has the effect of changing the balance of power on earth. Supernatural powers opposing frail humanity no longer dominate, where heaven has a conduit through which to speak into the human heart.

> *Luke 11:14 (NKJV) — 14 And He was casting out a demon, and it was mute. So it was, when the demon had gone out, that the mute spoke; and the multitudes marveled.*

The seeing prophet can relay God's plan, applying the keys, by opening up the revelation of heaven and through a power encounter, bringing people into the experience of liberty.

Jesus performed amazing miracles at times, signalling where his authority and power was from. On one occasion he used demonstrative prophecy in the form of sign language to speak to a deaf and mute man. He communicated with the deaf and mute man

---

[167] keys of David Rev 3:7; Keys of death and hades rev 1:18

through touching his deaf ears and looking upwards, indicating where his source of power came from. He also communicated with the onlookers by speaking out loud, so that they could also understand what he was about to do.

> *Mark 7:31-37 Then Jesus left the vicinity of Tyre and went through Sidon, down to the Sea of Galilee and into the region of the Decapolis. [32] There some people brought to him a man who was deaf and could hardly talk, and they begged him to place his hand on the man. [33] After he took him aside, away from the crowd, Jesus put his fingers into the man's ears. Then he spit and touched the man's tongue. [34] He looked up to heaven and with a deep sigh said to him,* **"Ephphatha!"** *(which means,* **"Be opened!"***). [35] At this, the man's ears were opened, his tongue was loosened, and he began to speak plainly. [36] Jesus commanded them not to tell anyone. But the more he did so, the more they kept talking about it. [37] People were overwhelmed with amazement. "He has done everything well," they said. "He even makes the deaf hear, and the mute speak."*

Prophets are well placed to demonstrate the gift of miracles, just as they were in the Old Testament. Indeed, as Bill Johnson would say, "you have not fully preached the gospel if you have not preached signs and wonders"[168].

The Expectation of our Ancestors

This present conviction of the presence of heaven is a dramatic change in fortunes. Our fathers and mothers have in the past been more mindful of the gap between heaven and earth, rather than the bridge that now connects them. For people in the Old Testament, the

---

[168] Romans 15:19–20 (NKJV) — 19 in mighty signs and wonders, by the power of the Spirit of God, so that from Jerusalem and round about to Illyricum I have fully preached the gospel of Christ. 20 And so I have made it my aim to preach the gospel, not where Christ was named, lest I should build on another man's foundation,

gulf between heaven and earth was seen as very great.[169] They viewed it in mainly physical terms. Heaven was easily represented by the creation above them, that is the sky, the earth below being affected by divine temperament.

> *2 Samuel 22:8 (NKJV) — 8 "Then the earth shook and trembled; The foundations of heaven quaked and were shaken, Because He was angry.; Job 26:11 (NKJV) — 11 The pillars of heaven tremble, And are astonished at His rebuke.*

When his favour comes, the rain descends as a blessing on earth, as does the manna[170]. So, our fathers and mothers looked towards the heavens, encouraged by God to dream and to hope.[171] In the spiritual sense, heaven was the realm of God. More otherworldly and distant, and so God's thoughts were so much loftier and impossible to attain.[172]

We, however, have no such barriers to the presence of heaven, we have an invitation to sit in heavenly places. But for our ancestors, the physical and spiritual universe, as seen in the pattern set by earth and sky, were altogether separate and distant.[173]

---

[169] Both in the physical and spiritual sense a The Hebrew word translated "heaven" or "the heavens" is $\sigma\eta\alpha 4\mu\alpha\psi\iota\mu$, "lofty"),. It is used in two primary senses. The spiritual and physical senses of heaven

[170] Psalm 78:23-24

[171] We find such expressions as "toward the heavens," "reaching to heaven" (Ge 15:5; 28:12); "under heaven," i.e., on earth (Ec 1:13; 2:3); "under the $\eta\varepsilon\alpha\varpi\varepsilon\nu\sigma$, [] i.e., the whole earth (Ge 7:19; Dt 2:25; Job 28:24 ; etc.); "the heavens and the earth," (Ge 1:1; 2:1).

[172] "'For my thoughts are not your thoughts, neither are my ways your ways,' declares the LORD. 'As the heavens are higher than the earth, so are my ways higher than your ways and my thoughts than your thoughts' " (Isaiah 55:8-9).

[173] Job 37:16; Job 36:28; Pr 3:20; Ps 78:23 ; cf. Isa 45:8; (Ps 77:17-18).

The believer has an ability, through proper and prophetic use of the keys of the kingdom given by Father, to unlock bondages and oppression; to bring heaven to bear. The mature child unlocks circumstances and opens doors because they are their Father's children and know their Father's will.

The Prophetic Power of Agreement

"Lawlessness conspires to divorce man from the power inherent in agreement."

The problem we face in a sceptical age is that cynicism breaks down bridges of trust between people and puts up barriers which are virtually impossible to dismantle. It produces distrusting hearts, which are unable to submit to one another.

We are being systematically programmed to be distrusting of and reluctant to submit to rulers and authorities.[174] It is called the spirit of lawlessness, a power that is prophesied to grow in influence and power as we approach the end of the age. Consequentially the church needs to guard against this spirit, which is both divisive and unproductive.

This spirit has one goal in mind; to condition humanity, so that order in society is broken down and authority figures are not trusted, brother is divided against brother, and no one is believed. Yet the

---

[174] *1 Peter 2:13 (NKJV) — 13 Therefore submit yourselves to every ordinance of man for the Lord's sake, whether to the king as supreme,*

understanding of submission is critical to a healthy and spiritually victorious Christian life.[175]

Demonic forces know that man can build anything if they become united and work as one.[176] Agreement has a power and dynamism, which can itself become a self-fulfilling prophecy. If agreement is found, there will be times when the only limitations stopping the power of that agreement from achieving its objectives, will be the intervention of God himself. This is why so many people manage to accomplish outstanding objectives in this life. Agreement is a subset of the law of sowing and reaping, a law written by God into the very fabric of the universe .

---

[175] *James 4:7 (NKJV) — 7 Therefore submit to God. Resist the devil and he will flee from you.*

[176] *Genesis 11:1–9 (NKJV) — 1 Now the whole earth had one language and one speech. 2 And it came to pass, as they journeyed from the east, that they found a plain in the land of Shinar, and they dwelt there. 3 Then they said to one another, "Come, let us make bricks and bake them thoroughly." They had brick for stone, and they had asphalt for mortar. 4 And they said, "Come, let us build ourselves a city, and a tower whose top is in the heavens; let us make a name for ourselves, lest we be scattered abroad over the face of the whole earth." 5 But the LORD came down to see the city and the tower which the sons of men had built. 6 And the LORD said, "Indeed the people are one and they all have one language, and this is what they begin to do; now nothing that they propose to do will be withheld from them. 7 Come, let Us go down and there confuse their language, that they may not understand one another's speech." 8 So the LORD scattered them abroad from there over the face of all the earth, and they ceased building the city. 9 Therefore its name is called Babel, because there the LORD confused the language of all the earth; and from there the LORD scattered them abroad over the face of all the earth.*

The Demands of Prophetic Agreement

The story of the tower of Babel reveals that those who built it had a common speech, indicating a common culture.[177] They had common purpose, implying common vision. The prophetic demands a similar level of commitment. To build with God we need to dwell in heavenly places until heaven's culture becomes ours, and we share a common speech with heaven. Whilst the tower of Babel was an extraordinary achievement, with humanity showing an ability to work together as one, God would prefer to be foundational to the building process, and he wants to build with us. To that end, if we will listen, he will give us precise prophetic plans relevant to his purposes for our life.

Noah received such appropriate plans.[178] Whilst the purpose was not necessarily clear to those around Noah, he certainly understood that

---

[177] God uses Culture as a prophetic backdrop. (c/f) Exodus 12:25–27 (NKJV) — 25 It will come to pass when you come to the land which the LORD will give you, just as He promised, that you shall keep this service. 26 And it shall be, when your children say to you, 'What do you mean by this service?' 27 that you shall say, 'It is the Passover sacrifice of the LORD, who passed over the houses of the children of Israel in Egypt when He struck the Egyptians and delivered our households.'" So the people bowed their heads and worshiped.

[178] Genesis 6:11–21 (NKJV) — 11 The earth also was corrupt before God, and the earth was filled with violence. 12 So God looked upon the earth, and indeed it was corrupt; for all flesh had corrupted their way on the earth. 13 And God said to Noah, "The end of all flesh has come before Me, for the earth is filled with violence through them; and behold, I will destroy them with the earth. 14 Make yourself an ark of gopherwood; make rooms in the ark, and cover it inside and outside with pitch. 15 And this is how you shall make it: The length of the ark shall be three hundred cubits, its width fifty cubits, and its height thirty cubits. 16 You shall make a window for the ark, and you shall finish it to a cubit from above; and set the door of the ark in its side. You shall make it with lower, second, and third decks. 17 And behold, I Myself am bringing floodwaters on the earth, to destroy from under heaven all flesh in which is the breath of life; everything that is on the earth shall die. 18 But I will establish My covenant with you; and you shall go into the ark—you, your sons, your wife, and your sons' wives with you. 19 And of every living thing of all flesh you shall bring two of every sort into the ark, to keep them alive with you; they shall be male and female. 20 Of the birds after their kind, of animals after their kind, and of every creeping thing of the earth after its kind, two of every kind will come to you to keep them alive. 21 And you shall take for yourself of all food that is eaten, and you shall gather it to yourself; and it shall be food for you and for them."

God wanted to rescue him and his family from the wrath that was to come in the form of a flood.

From Noah's story, we gain insight into how God builds. The Ark was built over a long period of time in which Noah demonstrated trust. God builds progressively, and the story of humanity is the story of relationships built on the foundations of previous generations. All true spiritual growth reflects similar qualities, it comes in stages and is a journey, which has foundations upon which it rests.[179] God builds the church on foundations of apostles and prophets.[180] The consistent Christian's walk is built on the foundation of faith and prayer.[181] Since the very universe is founded on his word, it is not surprising that Christian life should be founded on his word, if inconsistencies and cracks emerge in a believer's life, first query the strength of the foundations.[182] How deep do they go and how well were they laid? [183]

---

[179] *1 Corinthians 3:10–14 (NKJV) — 10 According to the grace of God which was given to me, as a wise master builder I have laid the foundation, and another builds on it. But let each one take heed how he builds on it. 11 For no other foundation can anyone lay than that which is laid, which is Jesus Christ. 12 Now if anyone builds on this foundation with gold, silver, precious stones, wood, hay, straw, 13 each one's work will become clear; for the Day will declare it, because it will be revealed by fire; and the fire will test each one's work, of what sort it is. 14 If anyone's work which he has built on it endures, he will receive a reward.*

[180] *Ephesians 2:20 (NKJV) — 20 having been built on the foundation of the apostles and prophets, Jesus Christ Himself being the chief cornerstone,*

[181] *Jude 20 (NKJV) — 20 But you, beloved, building yourselves up on your most holy faith, praying in the Holy Spirit,*

[182] *Luke 6:46–7:1 (NKJV) — 46 "But why do you call Me 'Lord, Lord,' and not do the things which I say? 47 Whoever comes to Me, and hears My sayings and does them, I will show you whom he is like: 48 He is like a man building a house, who dug deep and laid the foundation on the rock. And when the flood arose, the stream beat vehemently against that house, and could not shake it, for it was founded on the rock. 49 But he who heard and did nothing is like a man who built a house on the earth without a foundation, against which the stream beat vehemently; and immediately it fell. And the ruin of that house was great." 1 Now when He concluded all His sayings in the hearing of the people, He entered Capernaum.*

"The redemption of all things is the Father's purpose"

Success in spiritual life demands that we find the ability to work in a spirit of agreement because God primarily works in team. The future that God is building demands that we also acquire the humility to work without strong ego, to work in good fellowship, and the harness of team orders.

Yet there is still one clear vital hurdle to discovering the joy of working in agreement with others. If we are to commit in harmony to a body of people, we must first discern that they do indeed carry the word of the Lord, before any such commitment is made. If what we are joining to is not the word of the Lord, then we could find that it becomes a thorn in our life. Abraham tried to build a family, despite the fact that he knew that God had spoken to him and promised that he and Sarah would have a child. By collaborating with his wife Sarah to father a child with her maidservant,[184] rather than waiting for God to fulfil his promise, he agreed to pursue the dream outside the will of God. The result was Ishmael, father of Arabic people, who became a thorn in the side for his son Isaac and their descendants. The Jews and Arabs who are both descended from Abraham, have been in conflict ever since.

---

[183] *Acts 20:32 (NKJV)* — 32 "So now, brethren, I commend you to God and to the word of His grace, which is able to build you up and give you an inheritance among all those who are sanctified.

[184] *Genesis 16:1–3 (NKJV)* — 1 Now Sarai, Abram's wife, had borne him no children. And she had an Egyptian maidservant whose name was Hagar. 2 So Sarai said to Abram, "See now, the LORD has restrained me from bearing children. Please, go in to my maid; perhaps I shall obtain children by her." And Abram heeded the voice of Sarai. 3 Then Sarai, Abram's wife, took Hagar her maid, the Egyptian, and gave her to her husband Abram to be his wife, after Abram had dwelt ten years in the land of Canaan.

Agreement produces most fruit because it is a team exercise reflective of God's nature and therefore infused into every aspect of creation. Even at the beginning of a human life, that life is meant to come about through an act of loving agreement called lovemaking, resulting in the eventual birth of a child.

PROPHETIC AGREEMENT BUILDS THE CHURCH

To build church requires flexibility[185] in the wineskins. A flexibility in action and attitude is essential if we are to be tools Christ can use to shape and strengthen the church. Prophetic church building starts with increasing revelations of Christ.[186] All prophecy is infused with at least the subliminal testimony of Jesus, if not the blatant. Therefore, when we come to agreement over a prophecy, we are united in making Christ known. The quality of such spiritual intimacy and fervour is foundational to the building of the church.

We all know that church in its most basic form is the people. We also know that the height of revelation the church can receive, is of God's love for us in Christ. Therefore, prophecy foundationally is used by

---

[185] *Luke 5:37–39 (NKJV) — 37 And no one puts new wine into old wineskins; or else the new wine will burst the wineskins and be spilled, and the wineskins will be ruined. 38 But new wine must be put into new wineskins, and both are preserved. 39 And no one, having drunk old wine, immediately desires new; for he says, 'The old is better.' "*

[186] *Matthew 16:15–16 (NKJV) — 15 He said to them, "But who do you say that I am?" 16 Simon Peter answered and said, "You are the Christ, the Son of the living God." ; Matthew 18:16–20 (NKJV) — 16 But if he will not hear, take with you one or two more, that 'by the mouth of two or three witnesses every word may be established.' 17 And if he refuses to hear them, tell it to the church. But if he refuses even to hear the church, let him be to you like a heathen and a tax collector. 18 "Assuredly, I say to you, whatever you bind on earth will be bound in heaven, and whatever you loose on earth will be loosed in heaven. 19 "Again I say to you that if two of you agree on earth concerning anything that they ask, it will be done for them by My Father in heaven. 20 For where two or three are gathered together in My name, I am there in the midst of them."*

God to strengthen the relational bond between the saviour and the saved; between God and the believer. The building of the church from a prophetic perspective is the introduction of this love language of heaven; given to inspire the church to greater degrees of love, and to strengthen faith in those hearts in which the revelation is found; that the church becomes what it is meant to be, an undefeatable force.

Resistance to the prophetic word can come from the most unlikely of places. It is not just from external sources that opposition to the word comes. It is not just struggling disobedient Christians that can thwart the smooth journey of spiritual growth for a Christian community; our internal personal struggles and attitudes often present an even greater challenge to faith. Flippant and cheap intimacy is no substitute for genuine and reverent worship. Cheap intimacy is hallmarked by familiarity rather than respect, pride rather than humility, presumption rather than faith.[187] So Peter finds himself at the moment of his greatest revelation; the point at which he is left in no doubt that Jesus is the Christ, questioning the logic of Christ's determined visit to Jerusalem, disputing with the one about whom God gave him clarity of revelation. This happened just after the transfiguration where he was told, in the presence of the glory cloud by God himself, to listen to Christ and to lay down his agenda, clearly his opinions were at this point more important to him.

Personal ambition has to be confronted and curbed if revelation is to become a bridge to obedience rather than a cause of divine

---

[187] *Matthew 16:21–22 (NKJV) — 21 From that time Jesus began to show to His disciples that He must go to Jerusalem, and suffer many things from the elders and chief priests and scribes, and be killed, and be raised the third day. 22 Then Peter took Him aside and began to rebuke Him, saying, "Far be it from You, Lord; this shall not happen to You!"*

rejection,[188] somehow we must find the humility to put aside preferred interpretation in pursuit of the divine mind.[189] You can't build the church by intrigue.[190] Leaders then should foster an environment in which there are increasing revelations of Christ[191]. This facilitates the power of agreement, for Christ is the greatest unifying force in a body of believers, and in him we find agreement. He is not impressed by anything we build through self-effort, which reflects vanity.[192]

The prophetic then builds us together like bricks, which are difficult to separate. The Bible uses the Greek word "sunoikodomeo", which means "to build together",[193] to describe what God is metaphorically

---

[188] *Matthew 16:23 (NKJV) — 23 But He turned and said to Peter, "Get behind Me, Satan! You are an offense to Me, for you are not mindful of the things of God, but the things of men."*

[189] *Matthew 16:24–28 (NKJV) — 24 Then Jesus said to His disciples, "If anyone desires to come after Me, let him deny himself, and take up his cross, and follow Me. 25 For whoever desires to save his life will lose it, but whoever loses his life for My sake will find it. 26 For what profit is it to a man if he gains the whole world, and loses his own soul? Or what will a man give in exchange for his soul? 27 For the Son of Man will come in the glory of His Father with His angels, and then He will reward each according to his works. 28 Assuredly, I say to you, there are some standing here who shall not taste death till they see the Son of Man coming in His kingdom."*

[190] *Habakkuk 2:9–12 (NKJV) — 9 "Woe to him who covets evil gain for his house, That he may set his nest on high, That he may be delivered from the power of disaster! 10 You give shameful counsel to your house, Cutting off many peoples, And sin against your soul. 11 For the stone will cry out from the wall, And the beam from the timbers will answer it. 12 "Woe to him who builds a town with bloodshed, Who establishes a city by iniquity!*

[191] *1 Corinthians 14:12 (NKJV) — 12 Even so you, since you are zealous for spiritual gifts, let it be for the edification of the church that you seek to excel.*

[192] *Psalm 127:1 (NKJV) — 1 Unless the LORD builds the house, They labour in vain who build it; Unless the LORD guards the city, The watchman stays awake in vain.*

[193] *Ephesians 2:22 (NKJV) — 22 in whom you also are being built together for a dwelling place of God in the Spirit.*

doing with the church. God is not building what amounts to a theological college, full of head knowledge and information; rather he is building a family with a clear mission.

Regardless of how impressive the structure, unless the Lord is the architect it will eventually come to ruin.[194] Unless the Lord is involved in what we choose to build, then building becomes a strenuous burden and we could find, rather than the granting of an inheritance for sons and daughters, we may end up giving everything we have accumulated to someone else.[195]

---

[194] *Matthew 24:1–2 (NKJV) — 1 Then Jesus went out and departed from the temple, and His disciples came up to show Him the buildings of the temple. 2 And Jesus said to them, "Do you not see all these things? Assuredly, I say to you, not one stone shall be left here upon another, that shall not be thrown down."*

[195] *Luke 12:16–21 (NKJV) — 16 Then He spoke a parable to them, saying: "The ground of a certain rich man yielded plentifully. 17 And he thought within himself, saying, 'What shall I do, since I have no room to store my crops?' 18 So he said, 'I will do this: I will pull down my barns and build greater, and there I will store all my crops and my goods. 19 And I will say to my soul, "Soul, you have many goods laid up for many years; take your ease; eat, drink, and be merry." ' 20 But God said to him, 'Fool! This night your soul will be required of you; then whose will those things be which you have provided?' 21 "So is he who lays up treasure for himself, and is not rich toward God."*

THE COST OF BUILDING A PROPHETIC LIFESTYLE

Jesus cautions us to weigh up the cost of living in the prophetic wind of the spirit.[196] Working towards the fulfilment of a prophetic revelation is hard; back-breaking work at one level, [197] but a light and easy yoke at another[198].

However it feels on the journey, the fear of having to start again should never determine what we are willing to do in the journey of obedience. Human failure is not something to be feared, but embraced in humility, before God. It is essential to understand that in order to build with God, he may sometimes require that we are willing to start again. God himself sometimes has to start again and to

---

[196] *Luke 14:25–35 (NKJV) — 25 Now great multitudes went with Him. And He turned and said to them, 26 "If anyone comes to Me and does not hate his father and mother, wife and children, brothers and sisters, yes, and his own life also, he cannot be My disciple. 27 And whoever does not bear his cross and come after Me cannot be My disciple. 28 For which of you, intending to build a tower, does not sit down first and count the cost, whether he has enough to finish it—29 lest, after he has laid the foundation, and is not able to finish, all who see it begin to mock him, 30 saying, 'This man began to build and was not able to finish.' 31 Or what king, going to make war against another king, does not sit down first and consider whether he is able with ten thousand to meet him who comes against him with twenty thousand? 32 Or else, while the other is still a great way off, he sends a delegation and asks conditions of peace. 33 So likewise, whoever of you does not forsake all that he has cannot be My disciple. 34 "Salt is good; but if the salt has lost its flavour, how shall it be seasoned? 35 It is neither fit for the land nor for the dunghill, but men throw it out. He who has ears to hear, let him hear!"*

[197] *Isaiah 57:14–16 (NKJV) — 14 And one shall say, "Heap it up! Heap it up! Prepare the way, Take the stumbling block out of the way of My people." 15 For thus says the High and Lofty One Who inhabits eternity, whose name is Holy: "I dwell in the high and holy place, With him who has a contrite and humble spirit, To revive the spirit of the humble, And to revive the heart of the contrite ones. 16 For I will not contend forever, Nor will I always be angry; For the spirit would fail before Me, And the souls which I have made.*

[198] *Matthew 11:30 For my yoke is easy and my burden is light."*

rebuild.[199] Nehemiah was chosen for such a task; he was willing to take a prophetic commission to rebuild the walls of Jerusalem, a process in which he found himself reviled for two reasons; firstly, the enormity of the task and secondly the perceived quality of the work.[200] But Nehemiah was willing to face the challenge and to fight any battles that stood in the way of accomplishing his objectives.[201] Unfortunately, God sometimes can't find courageous hearts such as Nehemiah's, nor individuals willing to be a prophetic tool with which he can build.[202] But for those willing, there is the comfort in knowing that however hard the task, there is a day of fulfilment.[203]

---

[199] Acts 15:16–17 (NKJV) — 16 'After this I will return And will rebuild the tabernacle of David, which has fallen down; I will rebuild its ruins, And I will set it up; 17 So that the rest of mankind may seek the LORD, Even all the Gentiles who are called by My name, Says the LORD who does all these things.' ; Amos 9:10–12 (NKJV) — 10 All the sinners of My people shall die by the sword, Who say, 'The calamity shall not overtake nor confront us.' 11 "On that day I will raise up The tabernacle of David, which has fallen down, And repair its damages; I will raise up its ruins, And rebuild it as in the days of old; 12 That they may possess the remnant of Edom, And all the Gentiles who are called by My name," Says the LORD who does this thing.

[200] Nehemiah 4:3 (NKJV) — 3 Now Tobiah the Ammonite was beside him, and he said, "Whatever they build, if even a fox goes up on it, he will break down their stone wall."

[201] Nehemiah 4:17–18 (NKJV) — 17 Those who built on the wall, and those who carried burdens, loaded themselves so that with one hand they worked at construction, and with the other held a weapon. 18 Every one of the builders had his sword girded at his side as he built. And the one who sounded the trumpet was beside me.

[202] Ezekiel 22:29–31 (NKJV) — 29 The people of the land have used oppressions, committed robbery, and mistreated the poor and needy; and they wrongfully oppress the stranger. 30 So I sought for a man among them who would make a wall, and stand in the gap before Me on behalf of the land, that I should not destroy it; but I found no one. 31 Therefore I have poured out My indignation on them; I have consumed them with the fire of My wrath; and I have recompensed their deeds on their own heads," says the Lord GOD.

[203] Micah 7:10–12 (NKJV) — 10 Then she who is my enemy will see, And shame will cover her who said to me, "Where is the LORD your God?" My eyes will see her; Now she will be trampled down Like mud in the streets. 11 In the day when your walls are to be built, In that day the decree shall go far and wide. 12 In that day they shall come to you From Assyria and the fortified cities, From the fortress to the River, From sea to sea, And mountain to mountain.

Some of God's prophetic building plans are generational and may span scores of generations of the same family.[204] David and Solomon both had it in their hearts to build the temple of God, but it took Solomon's generation to see the dream fulfilled.[205]

---

[204] *Isaiah 22:9–11 (NKJV) — 9 You also saw the damage to the city of David, That it was great; And you gathered together the waters of the lower pool. 10 You numbered the houses of Jerusalem, And the houses you broke down To fortify the wall. 11 You also made a reservoir between the two walls For the water of the old pool. But you did not look to its Maker, Nor did you have respect for Him who fashioned it long ago.*

[205] *2 Chronicles 6:7–11 (NKJV) — 7 Now it was in the heart of my father David to build a temple for the name of the LORD God of Israel. 8 But the LORD said to my father David, 'Whereas it was in your heart to build a temple for My name, you did well in that it was in your heart. 9 Nevertheless you shall not build the temple, but your son who will come from your body, he shall build the temple for My name.' 10 So the LORD has fulfilled His word which He spoke, and I have filled the position of my father David, and sit on the throne of Israel, as the LORD promised; and I have built the temple for the name of the LORD God of Israel. 11 And there I have put the ark, in which is the covenant of the LORD which He made with the children of Israel."*

How to Interpret and Activate Prophetic Analogies

Participation in the Prophetic is Conditional

I used to worry about language which implied that it is possible to "miss the blessing", but now I realise that even Jesus used such language. God invites us to believe that he knows the plans he has for us. We are invited to have faith in him for our future. Of course, when prophets begin to use language that demands participation, a number of devices are deployed by the reluctant to offset the prophetic invitation.

For example, in such circumstances, prophets could be claimed to be using manipulative language; making people feel guilty. Another barrier to submitting to the prophetic voice is the spiritual argument, "I am just weighing it up"; and another device to resist the language of entering into the blessing is fear, the questioning of the prophetic voice in terms of theological correctness "is it truth"? Yet God himself uses the language of invitation to participate in blessing.[206]

As the king who prepared a banquet for his son discovered in Matthew 22, not everyone invited to enter into any fresh experience of renewal will want what God is pouring out, and so many will choose to decline the invitation.

Prophetic analogies of the kingdom represent the canvas from which the prophet works. Picture the scene; you visit a fruit farm that you intend to purchase and stoop down to sample some fruit, in the process you see an ancient crown made of pure gold just sticking up through the soil. Being an amateur archaeologist, you deduce that the farm must sit on an ancient Roman compound and so you purchase the farm. Later you discover that the crown was surrounded by many ancient Roman coins, which is exciting, and so you thank God that in ancient times many chose to keep treasure hidden in the ground because there were no real banks as we know or understand them

---

[206] *Matthew 22:2-13 (NIV) "The kingdom of heaven is like a king who prepared a wedding banquet for his son. [3] He sent his servants to those who had been invited to the banquet to tell them to come, but they refused to come. [4] "Then he sent some more servants and said, 'Tell those who have been invited that I have prepared my dinner: My oxen and fattened cattle have been butchered, and everything is ready. Come to the wedding banquet.' [5] "But they paid no attention and went off—one to his field, another to his business. [6] The rest seized his servants, mistreated them and killed them. [7] The king was enraged. He sent his army and destroyed those murderers and burned their city. [8] "Then he said to his servants, 'The wedding banquet is ready, but those I invited did not deserve to come. [9] Go to the street corners and invite to the banquet anyone you find.' [10] So the servants went out into the streets and gathered all the people they could find, both good and bad, and the wedding hall was filled with guests. [11] "But when the king came in to see the guests, he noticed a man there who was not wearing wedding clothes. [12] 'Friend,' he asked, 'how did you get in here without wedding clothes?' The man was speechless. [13] "Then the king told the attendants, 'Tie him hand and foot, and throw him outside, into the darkness, where there will be weeping and gnashing of teeth.'*

now. This is exactly what the kingdom is like.[207] You suddenly find it and just like the crown in our story; it is something of great value.

Every kingdom encounter causes a reassessment of all things considered precious; it presents a choice to the hearer to give up what he or she has, for what is being offered.[208] A kingdom encounter presents us with the opportunity to buy into what God is offering or decline it. For the rich young ruler, the gold he had glittered brighter than the glory he beheld. He preferred religion to the offer of a relationship; his possessions in preference to the offer of restoration. Yet all are invited to store up treasure in heaven in preference to the fool's gold on earth.[209]

In Matthew 6:20, Jesus is using a wordplay, *"treasure, not treasure"* to challenge the values of the heart. Given the fact that many houses in his day would have been made with mud, the prophetic voice in this passage calls for us to store up treasure where thieves could not dig

---

[207] *Matthew 13:44-46 (NIV) "The kingdom of heaven is like treasure hidden in a field. When a man found it, he hid it again, and then in his joy went and sold all he had and bought that field. [45] "Again, the kingdom of heaven is like a merchant looking for fine pearls. [46] When he found one of great value, he went away and sold everything he had and bought it. (c/f) Matthew 13:22 (NIV) The one who received the seed that fell among the thorns is the man who hears the word, but the worries of this life and the deceitfulness of wealth choke it, making it unfruitful. (c/f) 1 Timothy 6:9-10 (NIV) People who want to get rich fall into temptation and a trap and into many foolish and harmful desires that plunge men into ruin and destruction. [10] For the love of money is a root of all kinds of evil. Some people, eager for money, have wandered from the faith and pierced themselves with many griefs.*

[208] *Rich young ruler, Mat 19:21*

[209] *Matthew 6:19-24 (NIV) "Do not store up for yourselves treasures on earth, where moth and rust destroy, and where thieves break in and steal. [20] But store up for yourselves treasures in heaven, where moth and rust do not destroy, and where thieves do not break in and steal. [21] For where your treasure is, there your heart will be also. [22] "The eye is the lamp of the body. If your eyes are good, your whole body will be full of light. [23] But if your eyes are bad, your whole body will be full of darkness. If then the light within you is darkness, how great is that darkness! [24] "No one can serve two masters. Either he will hate the one and love the other, or he will be devoted to the one and despise the other. You cannot serve both God and Money.*

through to rob us; to choose to store our treasure up in the vaults of heaven. The Greeks interestingly enough, called burglars "mud diggers", as thieves would dig through the mud walls to get to the valuable items in those homes. All worldly treasure stores are affected by corrosive forces, such as inflation or devaluation of the wealth held, [210] but treasure in heaven is not affected by these forces. Therefore we should be single of eye, keeping our focus resolutely on heaven, worldly treasures should not become our master.

The Three Disciplines

Changing the outlook of the hearer is one of the key jobs of the prophet. Christ gives us many analogies to help us understand prophetic symbolism. In this chapter, we will look at some of these prophetic symbols and analogies, which through the three disciplines of acceptance, declaration and meditation, become pillars of faith within the human heart. Interpreting these requires a flexibility of heart and mind. The first of these is acceptance; which is such a simple word yet packed with much meaning. Acceptance is the attitude heaven is looking for in the face of a prophetic word, regardless of whether we understand what God is saying.

> *John 12:47-50 (NIV) "As for the person who hears my words but does not keep them, I do not judge him. For I did not come to judge the world, but to save it. [48] There is a judge for the one who rejects me and does not accept my words; that very word which I spoke will condemn him at the last day. [49] For I did not speak of my own accord, but the Father who sent me commanded me what to say and how to say it. [50] I know that his command leads to eternal life. So whatever I say is just what the Father has told me to say."*

---

[210] 1 Peter 1:3-4 (NIV) Praise be to the God and Father of our Lord Jesus Christ! In his great mercy he has given us new birth into a living hope through the resurrection of Jesus Christ from the dead, [4] and into an inheritance that can never perish, spoil or fade —kept in heaven for you,

The second and third are closely aligned; declaration and meditation. When Joshua took over from Moses, God told him to be strong and courageous, specifically commanding him not to let the book of the law depart from his mouth, to meditate on it day and night.[211] Joshua was to speak out, to verbalise the words of the book of the law. He was also to contemplate prayerfully what he was reading throughout the day and at times, during the watches of the night.

I remember memorising my first verses of scripture. I would write out a scripture and it would take me all week to really be able to memorise it. In the process of repeating it out loud, I would think about what I was memorising. I would pray and involve the Lord in my meditation, and he would give me relevant insight pertaining to my life. Because I simply included God in my meditation, he spoke deep into my heart, sometimes using obscure scriptures to illuminate relevant issues affecting my life. The promise of heaven is that those who meditate will be successful in everything they do.[212]

Declaration is a necessity in this process, the scripture says that in the beginning God said "let there be light"; God himself speaks out and verbalises. It is by his word that he creates. The process of declaration is, in fact, acting out or dramatising through words what God has said. The act of confessing out loudly is not just a regurgitation; it has spiritual power embedded in the act itself.

> *Romans 10:8-10 (NIV) But what does it say? "The word is near you; it is in your mouth and in your heart," that is, the word of faith we are proclaiming: [9] That if you confess with your mouth,*

---

[211] *Joshua 1: 6-9*

[212] *Psalm 1*

"Jesus is Lord," and believe in your heart that God raised him from the dead, you will be saved. [10] For it is with your heart that you believe and are justified, and it is with your mouth that you confess and are saved.

When we apply these three disciplines to any analogy of scripture, the principles they contain can be accessed and activated in our lives. We will look now at a number of analogies and the kind of places meditation on the prophetic can take us.

The Analogy of the Seed.

For example, if I was to quote the scripture

"The kingdom of heaven is like a man sowing good seed". [213]

I wonder what you would think this seed symbolises. To properly understand what is meant, we need to let go of preconceived ideas. Otherwise, we might mistakenly assume that the seed spoken of here is the word of God; whereas, in this context, it is rather the sons of

---

[213] *Matthew 13:24-30 (NIV) Jesus told them another parable: "The kingdom of heaven is like a man who sowed good seed in his field. [25] But while everyone was sleeping, his enemy came and sowed weeds among the wheat, and went away. [26] When the wheat sprouted and formed heads, then the weeds also appeared. [27] "The owner's servants came to him and said, 'Sir, didn't you sow good seed in your field? Where then did the weeds come from?' [28] "'An enemy did this,' he replied. "The servants asked him, 'Do you want us to go and pull them up?' [29] "'No,' he answered, 'because while you are pulling the weeds, you may root up the wheat with them. [30] Let both grow together until the harvest. At that time I will tell the harvesters: First collect the weeds and tie them in bundles to be burned; then gather the wheat and bring it into my barn.'"*

the kingdom.[214] In this prophetic analogy in Matthew 13, Jesus is speaking about his missional heart, through which he is determined to send sons of the kingdom into the world to bring in a harvest. As we begin to embrace this prophetic word and start to meditate on it, we realise that having any genuine relationship with Jesus will result in us acquiring his missional mindset.

Prophetic analogies should not be overworked or overstretched. This prophetic scripture generally speaks about the work of God in the life of every believer. By meditating on it, we give God an opportunity for the Holy Spirit to deposit faith into our hearts. We also learn from this passage that we should not to be overly concerned about the work of the enemy, but rather focus our energies on the activities of God. We are encouraged in this scripture to pay attention to divine action, rather than fix our gaze too eagerly on the other players in any prophetic drama. Our focus should not be on Satan and his activities of sewing sons of the evil one into the unfolding drama, but rather on God.

---

[214] *The Parable of the Weeds Explained Matthew 13:36-43 (NIV) Then he left the crowd and went into the house. His disciples came to him and said, "Explain to us the parable of the weeds in the field." [37] He answered, "The one who sowed the good seed is the Son of Man. [38] The field is the world, and the good seed stands for the sons of the kingdom. The weeds are the sons of the evil one, [39] and the enemy who sows them is the devil. The harvest is the end of the age, and the harvesters are angels. [40] "As the weeds are pulled up and burned in the fire, so it will be at the end of the age. [41] The Son of Man will send out his angels, and they will weed out of his kingdom everything that causes sin and all who do evil. [42] They will throw them into the fiery furnace, where there will be weeping and gnashing of teeth. [43] Then the righteous will shine like the sun in the kingdom of their Father. He who has ears, let him hear.*

"Don't focus on the weeds when you can focus on the flower that blooms"

In Matthew 13, we are encouraged to see that despite demonic activity, there will be a harvest at the end of the age producing eschatological hope, showing itself to be a function of prophetic vision.[215] The prophetic analogy above is seeking to build faith in the work of the Lord, rather than fear in the attacks of Satan.

The Analogy of the Mustard Seed

Christ himself has prophesied over us, saying that even if our faith is as small as a mustard seed, we will move mountains. [216] In this narrative, the prophetic emphasis is on the smallness of the size of the seed, not in the generative power of the seed. Interpretation is best done through meditation and in the presence of the Lord. Of course, a good number of commentaries can help, particularly where the writer is expressing his personal encounter with God, as opposed to simply laying down a theological framework. The theological framework tells us what the boundaries of Christian interpretation are, but the personal experience written down in commentary form, reveals to us how the Rhema or utterance of God has impacted the hearer.

In this case, Christ speaks about the mustard seed sized faith, not as a means of encouraging us to look at the regenerative power of the seed, but as something which can grow. What is extraordinary in this story, is the smallness of the seed. The statement "small as a mustard

---

[215] *Eschatological dominion, Dan 7:22-26; Seventh trumpet, Rev 11:2*

[216] *Mat 13:31-32*

seed" was a Middle Eastern proverb used to indicate the diminutive nature of something exceptionally and curiously small.[217] We digress when the focus is too firmly fixed on what our faith can do, rather than who enables our faith, or when we miss the point of who that faith is in. It is the one who activates the mustard seed size of faith that is truly remarkable and, what he can do with it is that is extraordinary.

The Analogy of Yeast

Another prophetic analogy which reminds us not to jump too quickly to conclusions about the meaning of a metaphor being used symbolically to depict a prophetic message, is seen in Christ's use of the word yeast. Yeast is normally used in scripture to denote evil.[218] Yet in Matthew 13:33 Jesus is instead pointing out the unstoppable nature of his kingdom growing, with such a ferocity that nothing could stop its growth.

The Analogy of the Lost Sheep

The prophetic voice calls the lost back into the fold; hence prophecy convicts unbelievers as well as believers.[219] The concept of judgement in the prophetic voice is merely an instrument to highlight the necessity of relationship with heaven. Heaven's mood is one of joy

---

[217] *(e.g., "faith as small as a mustard seed,")*

[218] *(e.g., Ex 12:15; Lev 2:11; 6:17; 10:12; Mt 16:6,11-12; Mk 8:15; Lk 12:1; 1Co 5:7-8; Ga 5:8-9).*

[219] *1 Corinthians 14:22-24 (NIV) Tongues, then, are a sign, not for believers but for unbelievers; prophecy, however, is for believers, not for unbelievers. [23] So if the whole church comes together and everyone speaks in tongues, and some who do not understand or some unbelievers come in, will they not say that you are out of your mind? [24] But if an unbeliever or someone who does not understand comes in while everybody is prophesying, he will be convinced by all that he is a sinner and will be judged by all,*

over the repentant; heaven's focus is on finding the lost. The context of this story below is of the lost coin, the lost sheep and the lost son.[220]

> *Luke 15:4-6 (NIV) "Suppose one of you has a hundred sheep and loses one of them. Does he not leave the ninety-nine in the open country and go after the lost sheep until he finds it? [5] And when he finds it, he joyfully puts it on his shoulders [6] and goes home. Then he calls his friends and neighbours together and says, 'Rejoice with me; I have found my lost sheep'."*

There are those who would paint the prophetic voice as a herald of doom, but I prefer to think of the prophetic voice as a dispenser of grace and mercy. For the prophet carries the message of eternal restoration, the demand not just for repentance but the offer of forgiveness.[221] When we hear prophetic voices that only ever condemn, we need to think carefully, because Father has a merciful heart.

The Analogy of the Increasing Kingdom

The true prophet sees all in the context of increase; the rule of Christ is increasing despite the revisionist's secular propaganda which declares that the church is diminishing. The kingdom of God is advancing. It started with John the Baptist as a metaphor for all the

---

[220] *(luke 15:4-24)*

[221] King who wanted to settle accounts - mat 18:21-22; (c/f) James 2:12-14 (NIV) Speak and act as those who are going to be judged by the law that gives freedom, [13] because judgment without mercy will be shown to anyone who has not been merciful. Mercy triumphs over judgment! [14] What good is it, my brothers, if a man claims to have faith but has no deeds? Can such faith save him? ; (c/f) Matthew 5:43-45 (NIV) "You have heard that it was said, 'Love your neighbour and hate your enemy.' [44] But I tell you: Love your enemies and pray for those who persecute you, [45] that you may be sons of your Father in heaven. He causes his sun to rise on the evil and the good, and sends rain on the righteous and the unrighteous.

Old Testament prophets; his life particularly signifying the inauguration of a more forceful phase of kingdom activity.

> *Matthew 11:11-14 (NIV) [11] I tell you the truth: Among those born of women there has not risen anyone greater than John the Baptist; yet he who is least in the kingdom of heaven is greater than he. [12] From the days of John the Baptist until now, <u>the kingdom of heaven has been forcefully advancing, and forceful men lay hold of it</u>. [13] For all the Prophets and the Law prophesied until John. [14] And if you are willing to accept it, he is the Elijah who was to come.*

We are humbled to know that the redemptive state in which we stand is clearly superior to any standing enjoyed by those who believed in God before Christ came, but what does it mean to say that "forceful men take a hold of it", meaning this kingdom? The political leaders wanted a political question answered; they resisted the charismatic movement that God was ushering in, as introduced by John, Jesus and the apostles. The will of God has always been frustrated, in the sense that despite tremendous evidences through miracles and other signs, man has often opposed that will.

The kingdom Christ is speaking of above is the final kingdom eschatologically promised, the rule of Christ, which has nothing to do with the political constructs of the world. We cannot take hold of it through military force; hence Christ's disciples were told on his arrest to lay down their swords. Political might will not win the day for us. The extent of our violence is only ever the violence of love, but if the kingdom is increasing, in what way can it be demonstrated that the kingdom is advancing?

The current propaganda is that the church is on the decline, a factor which may be felt most keenly where there is greater resistance to the gospel. But the word of God says the kingdom is advancing; which is the truth? If we take a numerical analysis of the church, we find some incredible statistics. Between 1900-1945 alone, the church increased numerically by 1300%; 70% of those who have ever been saved, have been saved since the 1900's (see endnote[i]). So, Jesus speaks about an advancing kingdom, declaring that the least in the kingdom is greater than John the Baptist.

Typical of human nature, whilst Jesus wants to speak about the least in the kingdom; the disciples want to know who the greatest is in the kingdom.

> *Matthew 18:1-4 (NIV) At that time the disciples came to Jesus and asked, "Who is the greatest in the kingdom of heaven?" [2] He called a little child and had him stand among them. [3] And he said: "I tell you the truth unless you change and become like little children, you will never enter the kingdom of heaven. [4] Therefore, whoever humbles himself like this child is the greatest in the kingdom of heaven.*

Christ highlights that his kingdom is to do with humility of our heart, and not prominence of office. It is an internal kingdom which must be internally activated because the kingdom is within you.

Prophetic analogies of the kingdom correspond to the tools utilised by the prophets to facilitate acceptance, meditation and declaration. Mastering analogical interpretation is good, but better still is mastering a listening ear; because we come with assumptions that could be wrong.

Eschatological Hope, The Manna of Renewal

THE BEDROCK OF RENEWAL

Prolific Prophecy

Prolific prophecy is a sign of renewal, and the context in which this manual is being written is the experience of renewal within our local church. There are clearly eschatological tones in the prophetic narrative being received by our community. The message of John the Baptist was an eschatological message, the Messiah was coming, and he was bringing heaven with him, and so everyone had to get themselves ready, because "the Kingdom of Heaven is near."

> *Matthew 3:1-3 (NIV) In those days John the Baptist came, preaching in the Desert of Judea [2] and saying, "Repent, for the kingdom of heaven is near." [3] This is he who was spoken of through the prophet Isaiah: "A voice of one calling in the desert, 'Prepare the way for the Lord, make straight paths for him.'"*

John the Baptist lived mindfully of heaven's proximity and as a result, prophesied its nearness. John was conversant with heaven; living in communion with God.[222] At the point of Christ's baptism, it is only because God speaks to him that he realises Christ is the Messiah.[223]

The reason behind John's reluctance to baptise Jesus was initially because of what he knew about Jesus' previous lifestyle. It wasn't until Father spoke to him from heaven that he realised he was the Messiah. John's message was a living, personal experience; heaven was near to him, so he prophesied about its coming.

> *"To be conversant with heaven is to understand the language of revelation, to be comfortable with the mysterious and to live in two worlds."*

Significant moments in history are happening all around us; it takes spiritual eyes to see the significance of a seemingly insignificant carpenter's son. It takes more than religious observance, it takes a conversation with heaven.

This invariably feeds our eschatological hope; time for us is no longer linear. We know that the fullness of this kingdom is not yet known or enjoyed by us on earth as it is in heaven. So, we look forward eagerly to that time when Jesus will come again from heaven and bring all

---

[222] *Matthew 3:13-17 (NIV) Then Jesus came from Galilee to the Jordan to be baptized by John. [14] But John tried to deter him, saying, "I need to be baptized by you, and do you come to me?" [15] Jesus replied, "Let it be so now; it is proper for us to do this to fulfil all righteousness." Then John consented. [16] As soon as Jesus was baptized, he went up out of the water. At that moment heaven was opened, and he saw the Spirit of God descending like a dove and lighting on him. [17] And a voice from heaven said, "This is my Son, whom I love; with him I am well pleased."*

[223] *John 1:33 (NIV) I would not have known him, except that the one who sent me to baptize with water told me, 'The man on whom you see the Spirit come down and remain is he who*

things to fullness. The degree to which this desire is present in the heart, is the degree to which renewal, as experienced by John the Baptist and many since, will manifest on earth. Eschatological hope feeds renewal.

Renewals then are foreshadows of a future moment in history when Christ will return, and the earth will experience a global awakening.[224] The early New Testament believers were full of eschatological hope,[225] which has fuelled the rapid spread of Christianity and all the supernatural revivals since that time.[226]

Cultivating a Heart for Jesus

There needs to be a determined and passionate rekindling of spiritual hunger for Christ; a fresh cry of Maranatha in the hearts of the believing community, a new sense of falling in love with Jesus. It matters little if it begins with a bit of froth, as long as it leads to deeper hunger for Christ, it will result in renewal.

---

[224] *1 Thessalonians 1:10 (NIV) and to wait for his Son from heaven, whom he raised from the dead —Jesus, who rescues us from the coming wrath. (c/f) 1 Thessalonians 4:16 (NIV) For the Lord himself will come down from heaven, with a loud command, with the voice of the archangel and with the trumpet call of God, and the dead in Christ will rise first. (c/f) 2 Thessalonians 1:7 (NIV) and give relief to you who are troubled, and to us as well. This will happen when the Lord Jesus is revealed from heaven in blazing fire with his powerful angels. (c/f)*

[225] *Acts 1:11 (NIV) "Men of Galilee," they said, "why do you stand here looking into the sky? This same Jesus, who has been taken from you into heaven, will come back in the same way you have seen him go into heaven."*

[226] *Acts 10.*

PROPHECY OPENS UP WELLS OF RENEWAL

Streams of Living Water

> *John 7:37-39 On the last and greatest day of the Feast, Jesus stood and said in a loud voice, "If anyone is thirsty, let him come to me and drink. 38 Whoever believes in me, as the Scripture has said, streams of living water will flow from within him." 39 By this he meant the Spirit, whom those who believed in him were later to receive. Up to that time the Spirit had not been given, since Jesus had not yet been glorified. NIV*

John the Baptist, in speaking of Christ, told us that when he came, he would baptise with the Holy Spirit and with fire.

The coming of the spirit signifies very specific promises. The Spirit's presence would remind us of what Christ had said to his disciples; tell of what is to come, convict of sin and empower. His activity in the hearts of men would result in a stream of supernatural activity.

"Don't settle for religion when you can have renewal."

The prophetic is like a well in a desert. In hearing God, the soul drinks and lives.[227] The invitation of heaven is to cultivate that deep thirst for

---

[227] Isaiah 55:1-6 "Come, all you who are thirsty, come to the waters; and you who have no money, come, buy and eat! Come, buy wine and milk without money and without cost. 2 Why spend money on what is not bread, and your labour on what does not satisfy? Listen, listen to me, and eat what is good, and your soul will delight in the richest of fare. 3 Give ear and come to me; hear me, that your soul may live. I will make an everlasting covenant with you, my faithful love promised to David. 4 See, I have made him a witness to the peoples, a leader and commander of the peoples. 5 Surely you will summon nations you know not, and nations that do not know you will hasten to you, because of the LORD your God, the Holy One of Israel, for he has endowed you with splendour." 6 Seek the LORD while he may be found; call on him while he is near. NIV

God.[228] Spirituality is to be ever in the ascendancy, and once spiritual ecstasy is tasted, like the sweetest waters, it can never be forgotten.

David once longed for the taste of natural water from a well he used to drink from before he faced an enemy occupation, once tasted it could not be forgotten.[229] Once spiritual renewal is tasted it can never be forgotten, for it refreshes the spirit of a man.

---

[228] *Psalms 42:1-2 As the deer pants for streams of water, so my soul pants for you, O God. 2 My soul thirsts for God, for the living God. When can I go and meet with God? NIV*

[229] *1 Chronicles 11:16-20 At that time David was in the stronghold, and the Philistine garrison was at Bethlehem. 17 David longed for water and said, "Oh, that someone would get me a drink of water from the well near the gate of Bethlehem!" 18 So the Three broke through the Philistine lines, drew water from the well near the gate of Bethlehem and carried it back to David. But he refused to drink it; instead, he poured it out before the LORD. 19 "God forbid that I should do this!" he said. "Should I drink the blood of these men who went at the risk of their lives?" Because they risked their lives to bring it back, David would not drink it. Such were the exploits of the three mighty men. 20 Abishai the brother of Joab was chief of the Three. He raised his spear against three hundred men, whom he killed, and so he became as famous as the Three. NIV*

"Don't settle for a drink when you can have a river."

Jacob's well had been a source of water for countless people and over hundreds of years.[230] On one occasion, Christ stopped at this well while tired during a journey and began to minister to a woman who he found there.[231] His intention was to awaken her spirit to the possibility of drinking from supernatural waters, as provided by the Holy Spirit. Just as the seed needs the land to be watered in order to break through the soil, supernatural breakthrough is a consequence

---

[230] *John 4:3-15 When the Lord learned of this, he left Judea and went back once more to Galilee. 4 Now he had to go through Samaria. 5 So he came to a town in Samaria called Sychar, near the plot of ground Jacob had given to his son Joseph. 6 Jacob's well was there, and Jesus, tired as he was from the journey, sat down by the well. It was about the sixth hour. 7 When a Samaritan woman came to draw water, Jesus said to her, "Will you give me a drink?" 8 (His disciples had gone into the town to buy food.) 9 The Samaritan woman said to him, "You are a Jew and I am a Samaritan woman. How can you ask me for a drink?" (For Jews do not associate with Samaritans.) 10 Jesus answered her, "If you knew the gift of God and who it is that asks you for a drink, you would have asked him and he would have given you living water." 11 "Sir," the woman said, "you have nothing to draw with and the well is deep. Where can you get this living water? 12 Are you greater than our father Jacob, who gave us the well and drank from it himself, as did also his sons and his flocks and herds?" 13 Jesus answered, "Everyone who drinks this water will be thirsty again, 14 but whoever drinks the water I give him will never thirst. Indeed, the water I give him will become in him a spring of water welling up to eternal life." 15 The woman said to him, "Sir, give me this water so that I won't get thirsty and have to keep coming here to draw water." NIV*

[231] *Matthew 11:28 "Come to me, all you who are weary and burdened, and I will give you rest. NIV (c/f) Revelation 2:3 You have persevered and have endured hardships for my name, and have not grown weary. (c/f) kopiao, "to grow weary, be beaten out" (kopos, "a beating, toil"). (c/f) Tiredness in scripture can refer to a person being faint or sick. kamno, "to be weary," is rendered "to be weary" in Hebrews 12:3 Consider him who endured such opposition from sinful men, so that you will not grow weary and lose heart. NIV*

of the parched land being watered by the Spirit.[232] It is this water that we are invited to long for, as a source of our spiritual energy. If we have any spiritual heroes, men and women we have cherished in the recent past, or in the antiquities of church history, we can be sure that they drank from the same spiritual waters provided by Christ.[233] Natural wells are dug because of the most basic of human needs, the need to drink; spiritual wells are dug for that same reason.

Blocked Wells

When wells are blocked they can become stagnant pools; worse still, they can become broken cisterns which can no longer hold water.[234]

---

[232] *Isaiah 35 1-10 The desert and the parched land will be glad; the wilderness will rejoice and blossom. Like the crocus, 2 it will burst into bloom; it will rejoice greatly and shout for joy. The glory of Lebanon will be given to it, the splendour of Carmel and Sharon; they will see the glory of the LORD, the splendour of our God. 3 Strengthen the feeble hands, steady the knees that give way; 4 say to those with fearful hearts, "Be strong, do not fear; your God will come, he will come with vengeance; with divine retribution he will come to save you." 5 Then will the eyes of the blind be opened and the ears of the deaf unstopped. 6 Then will the lame leap like a deer, and the mute tongue shout for joy. Water will gush forth in the wilderness and streams in the desert. 7 The burning sand will become a pool, the thirsty ground bubbling springs. In the haunts where jackals once lay, grass and reeds and papyrus will grow. 8 And a highway will be there; it will be called the Way of Holiness. The unclean will not journey on it; it will be for those who walk in that Way; wicked fools will not go about on it. 9 No lion will be there, nor will any ferocious beast get up on it; they will not be found there. But only the redeemed will walk there, 10 and the ransomed of the LORD will return. They will enter Zion with singing; everlasting joy will crown their heads. Gladness and joy will overtake them, and sorrow and sighing will flee away. NIV*

[233] *1 Corinthians 10:1-5 For I do not want you to be ignorant of the fact, brothers, that our forefathers were all under the cloud and that they all passed through the sea. 2 They were all baptized into Moses in the cloud and in the sea. 3 They all ate the same spiritual food 4 and drank the same spiritual drink; for they drank from the spiritual rock that accompanied them, and that rock was Christ. 5 Nevertheless, God was not pleased with most of them; their bodies were scattered over the desert.*

[234] *Jeremiah 2:12-14 Be appalled at this, O heavens, and shudder with great horror," declares the LORD. 13 "My people have committed two sins: They have forsaken me, the spring of living water, and have dug their own cisterns, broken cisterns that cannot hold water. 14 Is Israel a servant, a slave by birth? Why then has he become plunder?*

Straying from God brings us into a drought like state[235] and is akin to despising life itself.[236]

Just as natural wells run dry, the inner reservoirs of our personal spirituality can run dry through neglect. Even when we are in very favourable environments, let alone while we are not. In some locations like Palestine, the water almost vanishes during the summer drought. Some natural wells are not covered, because the soil in that area is not likely to drift and fill them up. Similarly, in some church environments, little can find its way into the spiritual life so as to pollute divine purpose, but desert wells are always covered because of shifting sands. They taper to a point so that the opening is easily closed in order to safeguard the life-preserving waters. Likewise, when the church environment is dry, everyone protects the spiritual life they currently possess and whatever wells exist are personal and covered over, rather than corporate and shared.

The culture in which spiritual life exists is important. If the culture is unsanctified, the waters are polluted, and the flow of the spirit can

---

[235] *Jeremiah 2:5-8 This is what the LORD says: "What fault did your fathers find in me, that they strayed so far from me? They followed worthless idols and became worthless themselves. 6 They did not ask, 'Where is the LORD, who brought us up out of Egypt and led us through the barren wilderness, through a land of deserts and rifts, a land of drought and darkness, a land where no one travels and no one lives?' 7 I brought you into a fertile land to eat its fruit and rich produce. But you came and defiled my land and made my inheritance detestable. 8 The priests did not ask, 'Where is the LORD?' Those who deal with the law did not know me; the leaders rebelled against me. The prophets prophesied by Baal, following worthless idols.*

[236] *Jeremiah 17:13 O LORD, the hope of Israel, all who forsake you will be put to shame. Those who turn away from you will be written in the dust because they have forsaken the LORD, the spring of living water.*

seemingly run dry through unsanctified attitudes such as envy.[237] Isaac found that his attempt to prosper was met with opposition, disputes and a lack of room for him to flourish. His response was admirable; he resolved to dig more wells until the scourge of the drought had lifted on his prospects. In the course of his difficulty, God appears to him and predicts future blessing. What does Isaac do in response to this wonderful news? - he builds an altar to the Lord and digs another well.[238] After all his opposition, he achieves his objective.

Metaphorically, dry wells are used for other purposes or left abandoned.[239] We can see the result of that in many Welsh villages that once had thriving church buildings, now left to ruin or long since abandoned. They have now become hotels, guest houses or even shops; no longer used for what was intended.

Another blockage to drinking once the need to drink has been identified, is the source of the water. Salt water and fresh water do not flow from the same source.[240] Having resolved the need to drink, the fear of drinking from polluted waters causes many to go thirsty

---

[237] *Genesis 26:12-15. 12 Isaac planted crops in that land and the same year reaped a hundredfold, because the LORD blessed him. 13 The man became rich, and his wealth continued to grow until he became very wealthy. 14 He had so many flocks and herds and servants that the Philistines envied him. 15 So all the wells that his father's servants had dug in the time of his father Abraham, the Philistines stopped up, filling them with earth. NIV*

[238] *Genesis 26:23-25 From there he went up to Beersheba. 24 That night the LORD appeared to him and said, "I am the God of your father Abraham. Do not be afraid, for I am with you; I will bless you and will increase the number of your descendants for the sake of my servant Abraham." 25 Isaac built an altar there and called on the name of the LORD. There he pitched his tent, and there his servants dug a well. NIV*

[239] *Jeremiah 38:6 So they took Jeremiah and put him into the cistern of Malkijah, the king's son, which was in the courtyard of the guard. They lowered Jeremiah by ropes into the cistern; it had no water in it, only mud, and Jeremiah sank down into the mud.*

[240] *James 3:11-12 Can both fresh water and salt water flow from the same spring? 12 My brothers, can a fig tree bear olives, or a grapevine bear figs? Neither can a salt spring produce fresh water.*

and remain parched. What source the water is from is the overriding question, the paralysing fear. If the invitation is to drink from the waters of sin,[241] then the reluctance would be warranted. But if the invitation is a drink of the Holy Spirit, then fear should not weigh down the human heart. I have not yet in my years of experiencing the Holy Spirit in different theological contexts, found my theology changed by any such encounter. But I have always found my attitudes and lifestyles challenged. I have always found my love for Jesus, and the Gospel renewed, but never yet have I found my theological views of baptism, the cross, or the necessity to be born again altered.[242] Fear leaves the thirsty parched.

Any genuine hunger and thirst for Christ or his spirit, will be satisfied. This is the promise of Christ himself; there is no other baptiser in the Holy Spirit other than Christ. If the heart is right toward God there is no need to fear, for there is no demon powerful enough to come between the Christ who wants to bless by means of the Holy Spirit, and the humble Christian heart seeking to be filled with God's Spirit. The Christian needs to believe Christ when he made the promise; that

---

[241] *Proverbs 5:15-23 Drink water from your own cistern, running water from your own well. 16 Should your springs overflow in the streets, your streams of water in the public squares? 17 Let them be yours alone, never to be shared with strangers. 18 May your fountain be blessed, and may you rejoice in the wife of your youth. 19 A loving doe, a graceful deer-- may her breasts satisfy you always, may you ever be captivated by her love. 20 Why be captivated, my son, by an adulteress? Why embrace the bosom of another man's wife? 21 For a man's ways are in full view of the LORD, and he examines all his paths. 22 The evil deeds of a wicked man ensnare him; the cords of his sin hold him fast. 23 He will die for lack of discipline, led astray by his own great folly.*

[242] *Colossians 1:3-5 3 We always thank God, the Father of our Lord Jesus Christ, when we pray for you, 4 because we have heard of your faith in Christ Jesus and of the love you have for all the saints- 5 the faith and love that spring from the hope that is stored up for you in heaven and that you have already heard about in the word of truth, the gospel NIV*

if anyone is thirsty, he will fill them.[243] Those who wait on the Lord will find that he will answer,[244] the rains will come and with them, the presence of heaven which changes the environment, even whilst we are consumed by tears.[245]

Leaders Should Dig Wells That Encourage Faith

The act of digging a well is a prophetic act. Leaders should dig wells; that is, create a culture of thirsting after God that the people who follow them can drink from.[246] It is a divine responsibility given to leaders; they should serve the people at the coal face of their needs.

---

[243] 2 Kings 3:12-18 Jehoshaphat said, "The word of the LORD is with him." So the king of Israel and Jehoshaphat and the king of Edom went down to him. 13 Elisha said to the king of Israel, "What do we have to do with each other? Go to the prophets of your father and the prophets of your mother." "No," the king of Israel answered, "because it was the LORD who called us three kings together to hand us over to Moab." 14 Elisha said, "As surely as the LORD Almighty lives, whom I serve, if I did not have respect for the presence of Jehoshaphat king of Judah, I would not look at you or even notice you. 15 But now bring me a harpist." While the harpist was playing, the hand of the LORD came upon Elisha 16 and he said, "This is what the LORD says: Make this valley full of ditches. 17 For this is what the LORD says: You will see neither wind nor rain, yet this valley will be filled with water, and you, your cattle and your other animals will drink. 18 This is an easy thing in the eyes of the LORD; he will also hand Moab over to you. 19 You will overthrow every fortified city and every major town. You will cut down every good tree, stop up all the springs, and ruin every good field with stones."

[244] James 5:7-10 Be patient, then, brothers, until the Lord's coming. See how the farmer waits for the land to yield its valuable crop and how patient he is for the autumn and spring rains. 8 You too, be patient and stand firm, because the Lord's coming is near. 9 Don't grumble against each other, brothers, or you will be judged. The Judge is standing at the door! 10 Brothers, as an example of patience in the face of suffering, take the prophets who spoke in the name of the Lord.

[245] Psalms 84:5-7 Blessed are those whose strength is in you, who have set their hearts on pilgrimage. 6 As they pass through the Valley of Baca, they make it a place of springs; the autumn rains also cover it with pools. 7 They go from strength to strength, till each appears before God in Zion. NIV

[246] Numbers 21:16-18 From there they continued on to Beer, the well where the LORD said to Moses, "Gather the people together and I will give them water." 17 Then Israel sang this song: "Spring up, O well! Sing about it, 18 about the well that the princes dug, that the nobles of the people sank-- the nobles with sceptres and staffs." Then they went from the desert to Mattanah, NIV

One could not ask a five-year-old child to plumb water from a well that was 60 feet deep; therefore leaders need to take appropriate action and provide spiritual resources that people can access; channels through which the community can be spiritually satisfied and grow. The community, on the other hand, needs to develop attitudes which are resistant to settling for less than God's best.

"Don't settle in a desert when the promised land is yours."

The people of God could have entered the Promised Land within two weeks but ended up wandering in circles for 40 years. If we are to avoid their mistakes, then we must not lose the compass of faith. Rather than walk in what they heard God say, they marched in circles. Faith leads in a straight line from A to B, fear circles the problem. Identify the problems that are holding you back. The believer must account for them and deal with them if they are not to become a hindrance to entering into the promises of God.

"Don't live in a pigsty when you can have a palace."

Who would choose to live in a pigsty? Adam and Eve lived in a perfect garden, yet the love of sin enticed them to abandon the beauty of the garden paradise for hard toil and labour. Sin draws us into life without God which compared to the paradise of Eden, is a pigsty.[247] The prodigal son literally chose to live a lifestyle of sin.[248] Because his culture determines that inheritance is a function of birth, not death, he could ask for his share of his father's inheritance. We all know how hard it is to build a fortune, yet he squandered his, ending up looking after pigs. Now there is nothing wrong with pigs if you're a farmer, but who eats pigswill?

Like the prodigal son, we sometimes do not recognise the kindness of the Father, and pride sometimes takes us away from the blessings and environment of God. Nebuchadnezzar carried a similar pride in

---

[247] *Romans 1:21-26 For although they knew God, they neither glorified him as God nor gave thanks to him, but their thinking became futile and their foolish hearts were darkened. 22 Although they claimed to be wise, they became fools 23 and exchanged the glory of the immortal God for images made to look like mortal man and birds and animals and reptiles. 24 Therefore God gave them over in the sinful desires of their hearts to sexual impurity for the degrading of their bodies with one another. 25 They exchanged the truth of God for a lie, and worshiped and served created things rather than the Creator-who is forever praised. Amen. 26 Because of this, God gave them over to shameful lusts. Even their women exchanged natural relations for unnatural ones. NIV*

[248] *Luke 15:11-16 Jesus continued: "There was a man who had two sons. 12 The younger one said to his father, `Father, give me my share of the estate.' So he divided his property between them. 13 "Not long after that, the younger son got together all he had, set off for a distant country and there squandered his wealth in wild living. 14 After he had spent everything, there was a severe famine in that whole country, and he began to be in need. 15 So he went and hired himself out to a citizen of that country, who sent him to his fields to feed pigs. 16 He longed to fill his stomach with the pods that the pigs were eating, but no one gave him anything.*

his heart, seeing himself through such proud eyes that resulted in God having to discipline him for his pride.[249]

When Elisha needed a miracle of provision, he prophesied the word of the Lord over what he had in his hands.[250] The God who provides manna in the desert will provide bread from heaven to all his hungry children. His heart is to prepare a table before us and to fill our cup until it is full and running over.

> *"Don't settle for a snack, when you can have a feast."*

We are invited to "taste and see that the Lord is good", a prophetic invitation, efficacious for eternity, his word being manna, heavenly food. To snack as believers, rather than to feast on God's provision, is not only discourteous, it is short-sighted. The invitation is to feast on

---

[249] Daniel 4:28-34 All this happened to King Nebuchadnezzar. 29 Twelve months later, as the king was walking on the roof of the royal palace of Babylon, 30 he said, "Is not this the great Babylon I have built as the royal residence, by my mighty power and for the glory of my majesty?" 31 The words were still on his lips when a voice came from heaven, "This is what is decreed for you, King Nebuchadnezzar: Your royal authority has been taken from you. 32 You will be driven away from people and will live with the wild animals; you will eat grass like cattle. Seven times will pass by for you until you acknowledge that the Most High is sovereign over the kingdoms of men and gives them to anyone he wishes." 33 Immediately what had been said about Nebuchadnezzar was fulfilled. He was driven away from people and ate grass like cattle. His body was drenched with the dew of heaven until his hair grew like the feathers of an eagle and his nails like the claws of a bird. 34 At the end of that time, I, Nebuchadnezzar, raised my eyes toward heaven, and my sanity was restored. Then I praised the Most High; I honoured and glorified him who lives forever. His dominion is an eternal dominion; his kingdom endures from generation to generation. NIV

[250] 2 Kings 4:42-44 42 A man came from Baal Shalishah, bringing the man of God twenty loaves of barley bread baked from the first ripe grain, along with some heads of new grain. "Give it to the people to eat," Elisha said. 43 "How can I set this before a hundred men?" his servant asked. But Elisha answered, "Give it to the people to eat. For this is what the LORD says: `They will eat and have some left over.'" 44 Then he set it before them, and they ate and had some left over, according to the word of the LORD.

God's word, a much more important discipline than the discipline of eating three meals a day.

Whenever prophetic utterance is heard, miracles are not far behind. Indeed, almost every New Testament miracle appears to be preceded with a prophetic statement before the miracle takes place. And so the woman with the issue of blood said to herself "if I just touch the hem of his garment I will be healed". I remember visiting a church in London one year. After preaching, the Lord gave me a prophetic word to pray for someone with asthma. When I went back to visit the church a year later, the person I prayed for was still living in the instantaneous healing he had received. Naaman received such a prophetic word from Elisha before his healing.[251] The commander of the king of Aram's army faced a bleak future because he had contracted leprosy. On hearing about Elisha, he set out for Israel, eventually finding his way to the prophet's door where he received the word of healing.

---

[251] *2 Kings 5:1-10 Now Naaman was commander of the army of the king of Aram. He was a great man in the sight of his master and highly regarded, because through him the LORD had given victory to Aram. He was a valiant soldier, but he had leprosy. 2 Now bands from Aram had gone out and had taken captive a young girl from Israel, and she served Naaman's wife. 3 She said to her mistress, "If only my master would see the prophet who is in Samaria! He would cure him of his leprosy." 4 Naaman went to his master and told him what the girl from Israel had said. 5 "By all means, go," the king of Aram replied. "I will send a letter to the king of Israel." So Naaman left, taking with him ten talents of silver, six thousand shekels of gold and ten sets of clothing. 6 The letter that he took to the king of Israel read: "With this letter I am sending my servant Naaman to you so that you may cure him of his leprosy." 7 As soon as the king of Israel read the letter, he tore his robes and said, "Am I God? Can I kill and bring back to life? Why does this fellow send someone to me to be cured of his leprosy? See how he is trying to pick a quarrel with me!" 8 When Elisha the man of God heard that the king of Israel had torn his robes, he sent him this message: "Why have you torn your robes? Have the man come to me and he will know that there is a prophet in Israel." 9 So Naaman went with his horses and chariots and stopped at the door of Elisha's house. 10 Elisha sent a messenger to say to him, "Go, wash yourself seven times in the Jordan, and your flesh will be restored and you will be cleansed." NIV*

"Don't settle in bondage when you can live in liberty."

Bondage is not just physical, it can take many shapes; such as mental, emotional, spiritual or financial. Financial bondage was experienced by Elisha's fellow prophet when he lost an axe head.[252] Having lost the axe head he had borrowed to the bottom of the Jordan, he faced the real possibility of becoming enslaved for a debt he could not repay. Elisha, through a prophetic act, returned the axe head, making it float to the surface. Whether we face financial difficulties, or turmoil of any kind; where we find bondage of any description, don't settle for it. Christ has a prophetic word which can bring liberty into your circumstance. As the scripture says, "it is for freedom that Christ has set us free".

Prolific prophecy then is a welcome sign, as it signals renewal. Leaders are to facilitate prophetic utterance as it is often the tool God uses to herald in renewals. We are not to settle for the desert, when rivers of living water are promised for the thirsty.

---

[252] 2 Kings 6:1-7 The company of the prophets said to Elisha, "Look, the place where we meet with you is too small for us. 2 Let us go to the Jordan, where each of us can get a pole; and let us build a place there for us to live." And he said, "Go." 3 Then one of them said, "Won't you please come with your servants?" "I will," Elisha replied. 4 And he went with them. They went to the Jordan and began to cut down trees. 5 As one of them was cutting down a tree, the iron axhead fell into the water. "Oh, my lord," he cried out, "it was borrowed!" 6 The man of God asked, "Where did it fall?" When he showed him the place, Elisha cut a stick and threw it there, and made the iron float. 7 "Lift it out," he said. Then the man reached out his hand and took it. NIV

Prophecy Challenges Values and Ministry

The personal challenge of prophecy is intense; when it comes, it will test the worldview of the one prophesying. Isaiah sees his call to a prophetic ministry as a personal challenge "I am a man of unclean lips". Prophetic insights bring a critical self-awareness, burning through the fog that obscures what lives in the heart of the prophet and exposes to him his own character. Prophecy challenges and tests the relational integrity we have with our heavenly Father.

Values and Ministry

What we see, understand, or experience, is filtered through the values that we hold. When we hear a testimony, it affects our behaviour as certainly as our response would be affected if, whilst attending a cinema, someone shouted fire! Whatever testimony we hear is measured against internally held values, and those internally held values provoke in us, as certain a reaction as we would display in a burning cinema auditorium. Our internal values affect how we respond to prophetic revelation.

In order to carry a prophetic message, scripture must first challenge the embedded perceptions we carry. The scriptures seek to shape those values and use a number of ways to encourage us to embrace the right kind of values; one of the devices the bible uses is comparison. The point of comparison from the supernatural point of view is to call for a rethink. Many for example, place a wrong emphasis on the utility of wealth, and consequentially denigrate the place of the poor.

What does one see when one looks at a poor man with dishevelled clothes? Are they valued by us, tolerated by us, loved by us? Godly values transcend the transitory nature of the material universe and comparison as a vehicle seeks to help us distinguish between eternal truth and the human condition.

Being poor does not devalue an individual; for one's financial situation has nothing of importance to say concerning the dignity or humanity of the poor. To help us understand this, scripture sets out a number of comparisons; for example, it compares relationships in the home which has frugal meals but is at peace, with a house full of feasting, but is also full of strife. It is not the amount of food at the table that matters, but the love that exists around it.[253]

Heaven advises that it is better in certain circumstances to be poor and maintain personal integrity, than to sear one's conscience by becoming rich through ill-gotten means.[254] We may envy the strong, but if strength and power wielded is out of control, it has no value. A powerful racing car has great power, but that power is of no value to it when, at one hundred and fifty miles per hour, the tyres lose

---

[253] *Proverbs 28:6 (LEB) — 6 Better to be poor and walking in one's integrity than to be crooked of ways when one is rich.; Proverbs 17:1 (LEB) — 1 Better a dry morsel and quiet with it than a house filled with feasts of strife.; Proverbs 15:16–17 (LEB) — 16 Better is little with the fear of Yahweh than great treasure and trouble with it. 17 Better is a dinner of vegetables when love is there than a fattened ox and hatred with it.*

[254] *Proverbs 16:19 (LEB) — 19 Better a lowly spirit with the poor than dividing the spoil with the proud.*

traction and the car is spinning out of control. In that scenario, power is of little value.

The comparison in scripture to a strong man with great power but lacking any emotional control, is the patient man who knows how to keep his temperament in check; he is in the long run, of greater value to society than a warrior.[255] Comparison is employed to highlight that it is preferable to share the company of a bear, than to share the company of a fool who revels in his folly.[256]

Values then transcend status and circumstances; you can have wonderful values that guide your life in the most difficult of circumstances because your values are what you aspire to. They are the internal signposts on the road of decision; the principles that govern our heart, and usually are most helpful when many choices confront us. Whilst common sense is useful, scripturally shaped values are most helpful.

Desires Confront our Values

> *1 John 2:15–17 (LEB) — 15 Do not love the world or the things in the world. If anyone loves the world, the love of the Father is not in him, 16 because everything that is in the world—the desire of the flesh and the desire of the eyes and the arrogance of material possessions—is not from the Father, but is from the world. 17 And the world is passing away, and its desire, but the one who does the will of God remains forever.*

Our desires lever the values that we hold. The prophetic can temper and restrain wrong desires because the prophetic life can resist the

---

[255] *Proverbs 16:32 (LEB) — 32 He who is slow to anger is better than him who is mighty, and he who controls his spirit than him who captures a city.*

[256] *Proverbs 17:12 (LEB) — 12 May a man meet a she-bear robbed of offspring and not a fool in his folly.*

seduction of the world which comes[257] in the form of its values and temptations.[258] Desires can scupper the noblest of stances. In 1 John the word Kosmos is being used comparatively, to highlight a twisted love of the world, in which desires have supplanted the place of affection God should occupy, a negative prioritising of affections.

> *"Eyes desire what eyes can see, God reveals what the spirit longs to see."*

The world competes for the love of Christians, and one cannot both love it and the Father, in equal measure. Put in absolute terms by John, "if anyone loves the world, the love of the Father is not in him."

James goes even further, asserting that *"Friendship with the world is hatred toward God" (Jam 4:4)*. Because Jesus lived, slept and walked in this world, fully engaged with it, we know that the lifestyle James demands does not advocate disengagement from the world. 1 John 2:17 goes to the heart of the challenge, which is the call to lay down the world's temporal offerings and embrace the divine will. So, we abstain from desires which war against our soul.

Prophetic utterance provides the means by which divine words can be programed into the human heart and open up the divine perspective on any set of values. When this happens, and our worldview becomes heavenly, we demonstrate that in every sense we are aliens and strangers in the world.

> 1 Peter 2:11–12 (LEB) — 11 Dear friends, I urge you as

---

[257] Jn 15:18-19; Jas 4:

[258] as opposed to the people who populate the world; other NT verses "world[κοσμοσ] means people, e.g., Jn 3:16-17

> *foreigners and temporary residents to abstain from fleshly desires which wage war against your soul, 12 maintaining your good conduct among the Gentiles, so that in the things in which they slander you as evildoers, by seeing your good deeds they may glorify God on the day of visitation.*

Perfect Values Stem from the Greatest Commandment

The greatest command is to love God with all our heart and soul and mind.[259] The second greatest commandment is to value and love your neighbour as yourself. If God comes first, then does my wife, family and children come second? Such human ways of coming to the question, or seeking to answer it, reveal how little understanding we have of God. He's not competing for the very affections he demands that we should devote to our family. What Jesus is in fact doing, is setting out an outline for experiencing and giving unconditional love.

We are truly only able to love our neighbour if we have first loved God. The world is full of hate, but Jesus teaches us to love our enemies and those who persecute us. Repeated acts of unconditional love confirm that you indeed love God with all your heart,[260] for no

---

[259] *Matthew 22:37–39 (LEB) — 37 And he said to him, " 'You shall love the Lord your God with all your heart and with all your soul and with all your mind.' 38 This is the greatest and first commandment. 39 And the second is like it: 'You shall love your neighbour as yourself.'*

[260] *Matthew 25:31–40 (LEB) — 31 Now when the Son of Man comes in his glory and all the angels with him, then he will sit on his glorious throne. 32 And all the nations will be gathered before him, and he will separate them from one another like a shepherd separates the sheep from the goats. 33 And he will place the sheep on his right and the goats on the left. 34 Then the king will say to those on his right, 'Come, you who are blessed by my Father. Inherit the kingdom prepared for you from the foundation of the world! 35 For I was hungry and you gave me something to eat, I was thirsty and you gave me something to drink, I was a stranger and you welcomed me as a guest, 36 I was naked and you clothed me, I was sick and you cared for me, I was in prison and you came to me.' 37 Then the righteous will answer him, saying, 'Lord, when did we see you hungry and feed you, or thirsty and give you something to drink? 38 And when did we see you a stranger and welcome you as a guest, or naked and clothe you? 39 And when did we see you sick or in prison and come to you?' 40 And the king will answer and say to them, 'Truly I say to you, in as much as you did it to one of the least of these brothers of mine, you did it to me.'*

one can truly love their neighbour unconditionally, except if they have first loved God. We understand what unconditional love looks like; "whilst we were yet sinners Christ died for us", and so unconditional love is primarily selfless.

Values based in love produce behaviour that leads to God being both glorified and proud of us. When we hear preaching that is full of hate and anger, we have to ask what values are underpinning such preaching, what roots are feeding the speaker's heart? Those who have been forgiven much, love much; the self-aware believer understands personal frailty.

The motivation behind our values at root is not a political one, nor is it an economic motivation, but rather the love of God in Christ. If our motivation behind our values is political, the politician gets the glory, but if it is rooted in the love of God, He gets the glory.

> *"When the heart is connected to God's love, every positive emotion becomes a subset of love rather than an orphan of the heart."*

Love is a prophetic tool which frames all our attitudes and all our values.[261] It draws honesty and integrity out of us effortlessly; a fruit of the spirit and catalyst for internal transformation.

Anger, even hatred, is changed into an emotion directed against the result of sin, rather than an unedifying attitude within the heart.

---

[261] *1 Corinthians 13*

When we love God,[262] more negative emotions can be transformed, being filtered through love by the spirit.[263] Because we love unconditionally, we are hard to refute and impossible to ignore. Whilst we uphold spiritually defined morality, we reject no man, while steadfastly presenting Heaven's, loving truth.

"Emotional effort disappears when love is the parent, for love draws out goodness."

Integrity within this revelation is no longer something to "work" at because love does not deal in hypocrisy. From a heavenly perspective, integrity is a function of love rather than just an aspiration of life. Our prophetic declarations are heard, whilst our lifestyles do not betray the message we herald. [264] Lack of integrity comes from an unclean heart.[265] There is a direct link between the content of the heart and the produce of the hands.[266] For a prophet, dealing with truth is not

---

[262] *Luke 14:25–27 (LEB) — 25 Now large crowds were going along with him, and he turned around and said to them, 26 "If anyone comes to me and does not hate his own father and mother and wife and children and brothers and sisters, and furthermore, even his own life, he cannot be my disciple. 27 Whoever does not carry his own cross and follow me cannot be my disciple.*

[263] *Galatians 5:22–23 (LEB) — 22 But the fruit of the Spirit is love, joy, peace, patience, kindness, goodness, faithfulness, 23 gentleness, self-control. Against such things there is no law.*

[264] *1 Corinthians 6:19–20 (LEB) — 19 Or do you not know that your body is the temple of the Holy Spirit who is in you, whom you have from God, and you are not your own? 20 For you were bought at a price; therefore glorify God with your body.*

[265] *Matthew 23:27–28 (LEB) — 27 "Woe to you, scribes and Pharisees—hypocrites!—because you are like whitewashed tombs which on the outside appear beautiful, but on the inside are full of the bones of the dead and of everything unclean! 28 In the same way, on the outside you also appear righteous to people, but inside you are full of hypocrisy and lawlessness.*

[266] *Galatians 6:7–8 (LEB) — 7 Do not be deceived: God is not to be mocked, for whatever a person sows, this he will also reap, 8 because the one who sows to his own flesh will reap corruption from the flesh, but the one who sows to the Spirit will reap eternal life from the Spirit.*

just about delivering it to others. A prophecy becomes a mirror of the soul, which demands that we deal with the cobwebs[267] of the heart if the message is to be received. The prophetic message to our generation then contains personal challenge for the prophet; it is a difficult place to live, for a prophet will never fit into a worldly context with ease.

Prophets speak through the ages and the generations, challenging the norms of the day. One of these norms is the current attitude towards sex outside of marriage. When romantic love is not an orphan of heaven's unconditional love, women are honoured in marriage, purity is revered, and submissiveness, mercy and good fruit are produced in sexual union. It is not just attitudes towards love that get a makeover; in the light of Christ, the New Testament prophet pursues peace instead of conflict.[268]

Yet still, other contemporary attitudes are challenged when love reigns supreme. No one who loves unconditionally can ever accept abortion as a legitimate choice, because the New Testament prophets are champions of life. The integrity of the prophetic message rejects any participation in the contrary spirit of death. No true Christian would ever condone abortion, for the spirit of Christ in them would resist such behaviour. It can only be done by ignoring the voice of

---

[267] 1 John 1:8 (LEB) — 8 If we say that we do not have sin, we deceive ourselves and the truth is not in us. ; 1 Peter 2:12 (LEB) — 12 maintaining your good conduct among the Gentiles, so that in the things in which they slander you as evildoers, by seeing your good deeds they may glorify God on the day of visitation.

[268] James 3:14–18 (LEB) — 14 But if you have bitter jealousy and selfish ambition in your hearts, do not boast and tell lies against the truth. 15 This is not the wisdom that comes down from above, but is earthly, unspiritual, demonic. 16 For where there is jealousy and selfish ambition, there is disorder and every evil practice. 17 But the wisdom from above is first pure, then peaceful, gentle, obedient, full of mercy and good fruits, non-judgmental, without hypocrisy, 18 And the fruit of righteousness is sown in peace among those who make peace.

God. The change in humanity that will see the end of 42,000,000 people aborted in the world every year, will come about by the pervasive change of culture that only the love of God can bring about. The prophetic voice breaks through, exposing the concept of choice when it comes to abortion as ultimately being a rejection of God's command to love.

Love senses and resists those things that corrupt innocent minds and provides a better narrative on life than the secular society has bought into. For culture is much like an orchestra, everyone works together in a form of unity and harmony in diversity.

The score in this metaphor stands for political correctness and, whilst there is a form of honour in the diversity of instruments and a sense of building together, the prophetic voice in this context sounds like discordant notes, but in heaven, it is heard in harmony with the angelic chorus. The prophetic voice must seek to change the culture of the church; its music, food, dress, and attitudes in order to reflect heaven's value, if it is going to challenge and change the culture in which it lives.[269] David demonstrated this kind of courage when he faced Goliath.

True prophets wash feet,[270] serving selflessly.[271] This is not Communism; the dream that scientific advancement and economic

---

[269] *Amos 5:24*

[270] *John 13:1–5 (LEB) — 1 Now before the feast of Passover, Jesus, knowing that his hour had come that he would depart from this world to the Father, and having loved his own in the world, loved them to the end. 2 And as a dinner was taking place, when the devil had already put into the heart of Judas son of Simon Iscariot that he should betray him, 3 because he knew that the Father had given him all things into his hands, and that he had come forth from God and was going away to God, 4 he got up from the dinner and took off his outer clothing, and taking a towel, tied it around himself. 5 Then he poured water into the washbasin and began to wash the feet of the disciples, and to wipe them dry with the towel which he had tied around himself.*

security can solve all man's difficulties, asserting the highest collective good, by denying the worth of the individual human personality. Values extend the human heart and through love, demonstrate the best in humanity.[272]

The values we hold particularly impact upon the ministries that have been written into our DNA by our Father, who we instinctively know, has written purpose into our lives.[273] Any self-respecting prophet knows that with a call to ministry comes conflict,[274] but our love

---

[271] *Acts 2:40–47 (LEB) — 40 And with many other words he solemnly urged and exhorted them, saying, "Be saved from this crooked generation!" 41 So those who accepted his message were baptized, and on that day about three thousand souls were added. 42 And they were devoting themselves to the teaching of the apostles and to fellowship, to the breaking of bread and to prayers. 43 And fear came on every soul, and many wonders and signs were being performed by the apostles. 44 And all who believed were in the same place, and had everything in common. 45 And they began selling their possessions and property, and distributing these things to all, to the degree that anyone had need. 46 And every day, devoting themselves to meeting with one purpose in the temple courts and breaking bread from house to house, they were eating their food with joy and simplicity of heart, 47 praising God and having favour with all the people. And the Lord was adding every day to the total of those who were being saved.*

[272] *1 John 3:17 (LEB) — 17 But whoever has the world's material possessions and observes his brother in need and shuts his heart against him, how does the love of God reside in him? ; 1 Timothy 6:17–19 (LEB) — 17 Command those who are rich in this present age not to be proud and not to put their hope in the uncertainty of riches, but in God, who provides us all things richly for enjoyment, 18 to do good, to be rich in good works, to be generous, sharing freely, 19 storing up for themselves a good foundation for the future, in order that they may take hold of what is truly life. ; Acts 20:35 (LEB) — 35 I have shown you with respect to all things that by working hard in this way it is necessary to help those who are in need, and to remember the words of the Lord Jesus that he himself said, "It is more blessed to give than to receive."*

[273] *Personal Transformation - Yinka Oyekan*

[274] *2 Corinthians 4:17–18 (LEB) — 17 For our momentary light affliction is producing in us an eternal weight of glory beyond all measure and proportion, 18 because we are not looking at what is seen, but what is not seen. For what is seen is temporary, but what is not seen is eternal.*

connection with our heavenly Father enables us to endure.[275] Ministry for us is not the striving for office[276] that accompanies the immature Christian. We know that a man can only receive what is given from heaven, and so we are content with that.

> *John 3:26–27 (LEB) — 26 And they came to John and said to him, "Rabbi, he who was with you on the other side of the Jordan, about whom you testified—look, this one is baptizing, and all are coming to him!" 27 John answered and said, "A man can receive not one thing unless it is granted to him from heaven!*

---

[275] 2 Corinthians 11:23–29 (LEB) — 23 Are they servants of Christ?—I am speaking as though I were beside myself—I am more so, with far greater labours, with far more imprisonments, with beatings to a much greater degree, in danger of death many times. 24 Five times I received at the hands of the Jews forty lashes less one. 25 Three times I was beaten with rods. Once I received a stoning. Three times I was shipwrecked. A day and a night I have spent in the deep water. 26 I have been on journeys many times, in dangers from rivers, in dangers from robbers, in dangers from my own people, in dangers from the Gentiles, in dangers in the city, in dangers in the wilderness, in dangers at sea, in dangers because of false brothers, 27 with toil and hardship, often in sleepless nights, with hunger and thirst, often going hungry, in cold and poorly clothed. 28 Apart from these external things, there is the pressure on me every day of the anxiety about all the churches. 29 Who is weak, and I am not weak? Who is caused to sin, and I do not burn with indignation?

[276] Matthew 20:20–28 (LEB) — 20 Then the mother of the sons of Zebedee came up to him with her sons, and kneeling down she asked something from him. 21 And he said to her, "What do you want?" She said to him, "Say that these two sons of mine may sit one at your right hand and one at your left in your kingdom." 22 But Jesus answered and said, "You do not know what you are asking! Are you able to drink the cup that I am about to drink?" They said to him, "We are able." 23 He said to them, "You will indeed drink my cup, but to sit at my right hand and at my left is not mine to grant, but is for those for whom it has been prepared by my Father." 24 And when the ten heard this, they were indignant concerning the two brothers. 25 But Jesus called them to himself and said, "You know that the rulers of the Gentiles lord it over them, and those in high positions exercise authority over them. 26 It will not be like this among you! But whoever wants to become great among you must be your servant, 27 and whoever wants to be most prominent among you must be your slave—28 just as the Son of Man did not come to be served, but to serve, and to give his life as a ransom for many."

Make the Most of Every Opportunity

Christians are not to be complacent about the opportunities that come our way. Someone once asked me the question "does God really want to speak to everyone's situation?", my response; which good father would not want to give the best advice to their children?

> *Ephesians 5:14–16 (LEB) — 14 for everything made visible is light. Therefore it says, Wake up, sleeper, and rise from the dead, and Christ will shine on you. 15 Therefore, consider carefully how you live, not as unwise but as wise, 16 making the most of the time because the days are evil.*

In this scripture, we are encouraged to focus on making the most of every opportunity, rather than the days which are evil. [277] We are encouraged to focus on God-given opportunities that stand out against the backdrop of the dark days in which we live. The darkness of the days are not what should occupy, or grip our attention, but the opportunities that Christ reveals to us.

"In light shadows vanish, in darkness light shows the way."

---

[277] Psalm 90:12 (LEB) — 12 So teach us to number our days that we may gain a heart of wisdom.

Now we have all met the pessimist who can only ever see the looming disaster; the problems that will beset, and the rain that's going to fall, on the planned picnic. A despondent and negative disposition is something that blinds to what is possible in Christ. It narrows circles of relationships and isolates from divinely offered blessings.

Every occasion presenting itself is to be seen for its potential to give glory to God. It is through prayer that the door to spiritual sensitivity and awareness is developed.[278]

To take every opportunity, the believer must wake up from his complacent form of Christianity,[279] we must wake up from our spiritual slumber.[280] The problems with the night and a lack of clear spiritual light, are that no one can see clearly enough to work effectively.[281] The night becomes a prophetic metaphor for an

---

[278] *Ephesians 6:15-18 and with your feet fitted with the readiness that comes from the gospel of peace. 16 In addition to all this, take up the shield of faith, with which you can extinguish all the flaming arrows of the evil one. 17 Take the helmet of salvation and the sword of the Spirit, which is the word of God. 18 And pray in the Spirit on all occasions (kairos) with all kinds of prayers and requests. With this in mind, be alert and always keep on praying for all the saints.*

[279] *Colossians 4:5–6 (LEB) — 5 Live with wisdom toward those outside, making the most of the time. 6 Let your speech always be with grace, seasoned with salt, so that you may know how it is necessary for you to answer each one.*

[280] *Romans 13:9–11 (LEB) — 9 For the commandments, "You shall not commit adultery, you shall not commit murder, you shall not steal, you shall not covet," and if there is any other commandment, are summed up in this statement: "You shall love your neighbour as yourself." 10 Love does not commit evil against a neighbour. Therefore love is the fulfilment of the law. 11 And do this because you know the time, that it is already the hour for you to wake up from sleep. For our salvation is nearer now than when we believed.*

[281] *John 9:3–5 (LEB) — 3 Jesus replied, "Neither this man sinned nor his parents, but it happened so that the works of God could be revealed in him. 4 It is necessary for us to do the deeds of the one who sent me while it is day; night is coming, when no one can work! 5 While I am in the world, I am the light of the world."*

inability to act, for not being able to find a way through the darkness.[282]

Worse still, a lack of spiritual light produces fear. Satan, we are told works in the darkness, blinding the mind of the unbeliever; sometimes, threatening with the valley of the shadow of death. Yet, whilst there is still hope in the human breast, courage holds out that one day, deliverance will come from the hand of God, and so we boast about his unfailing love to anyone who would care to listen.

We dream about the day we will meet the man or woman of our prayers and dreams; we hope we will be given the job opportunity we have prepared for, the ministry breakthrough we have prayed for, the family we have cried for. We long for the opportunity in all these things, to simply demonstrate a quality of love that brings glory to God. Prophecy brings God's light into those difficult situations.

> *"The prophet accesses prophecies already declared as these have pre-determined outcomes."*

We're not to just sit and hope, but to create pathways of hope in people's lives. We are a people who have the mandate to prophesy

---

[282] *John 12:35 (LEB) — 35 So Jesus said to them, "Yet a little time the light is with you! Walk while you have the light, so that the darkness does not overtake you! And the one who walks in the darkness does not know where he is going. ; Isaiah 59:9–10 (LEB) — 9 Therefore justice is far from us, and righteousness does not reach us. We wait for light, but look! there is darkness; for brightness, but we walk in darkness. 10 We grope like the blind along a wall, and we grope as without eyes. We stumble at noon as in the twilight; among the strong we are like the dead.*

transformational change into every situation.[283] In Hebraic thought, time is perceived of in terms of an appointed time, the right time, or the right opportunity. All this has been carried over into the New Testament word Kairos.[284]

What is important, is that the prophetic revelation and promises concerning the season we are in can be accessed now. Some prophetic statements are eternally flowing words, activated until at least the time of the return of Christ.

There are future "times", moments in history, infused with God-given purpose; supernatural seasons appointed by heaven in which things that are bound to happen must take place, soliciting constant prayer.[285] But also excitingly, for the discerning prophet there are moments right now when already given prophecy can be implemented.

For example, every simple act of evangelism has determined consequences if you proclaim it to a wide enough audience. Christ predicted that the outcome will be, some of those who hear will

---

[283] *Isaiah 61:1–3 (LEB) — 1 The Spirit of the Lord Yahweh is upon me, because Yahweh has anointed me, he has sent me to bring good news to the oppressed, to bind up the broken-hearted, to proclaim release to the captives and liberation to those who are bound, 2 to proclaim the year of Yahweh's favour, and our God's day of vengeance, to comfort all those in mourning, 3 to give for those in mourning in Zion, to give them a head wrap instead of ashes, the oil of joy instead of mourning, a garment of praise instead of a faint spirit. And they will be called oaks of righteousness, the planting of Yahweh, to show his glory.*

[284] *the Greek word "kairos is translated as " season, time, opportunity, occasion" to mean a moment or period in time, a point in time mat 13:30, It can be the capacity or potential Gal 6:7-10, or even our ultimate destiny (Mat 26:18) / The word Chronos marks the beginning and end of a period (acts 7:17; acts 4:4) whilst karios marks out what is possible in that season or timeframe (Mat 16:1-3 ; Mat 21:34)*

[285] *Ephesians 6:18 (LEB) — 18 with all prayer and supplication praying at all times in the Spirit, and to this end being alert with all perseverance and supplication for all the saints,*

receive the word and be saved,[286] 30, 60 even 100 percent of those who hear will turn to Christ. All throughout scripture determined outcomes are prophesied, whether they be the consequence of an action, the simple change of the weather,[287] or the result of harvest after sowing.[288]

There are determined spiritual outcomes which are also bound to happen. Those Pharisees who could not discern the spiritual season they were in, were called hypocrites.[289]

To elevate our gaze from the security of religious observance is the first step towards true discernment of the spiritual seasons. If we are

---

[286] Luke 8:13 (LEB) — 13 And those on the rock are those who receive the word with joy when they hear it, and these do not have enough root, who believe for a time and in a time of testing fall away.

[287] Mat 16:1-3 The Pharisees and Sadducees came to Jesus and tested him by asking him to show them a sign from heaven. {2} He replied, "When evening comes, you say, 'It will be fair weather, for the sky is red,' {3} and in the morning, 'Today it will be stormy, for the sky is red and overcast.' You know how to interpret the appearance of the sky, but you cannot interpret the signs of the times (kairos). (NIV)

[288] Matthew 21:34 (LEB) — 34 And when the season of fruit drew near, he sent his slaves to the tenant farmers to collect his fruit.

[289] Luke 12:56 (LEB) — 56 Hypocrites! You know how to evaluate the appearance of the earth and the sky, but how is it you do not know how to evaluate this present time?

not to become like the Pharisees,[290] our confidence must not be in the performance of duty. A lack of ability to discern the visitation of God speaks more about the lack of intimate fellowship than it does the lack of theological knowledge.

How do we discern the supernatural season? The spirit within us speaks to us as he did to the prophets of old. By fixing our minds and eyes on Jesus, we can download the divine will, either through the Word of God, or by the Rhema of God. We develop the mental discipline of remembering that Christ is involved in every aspect of life. We may be able through rational intuition, to work a number of things out, but natural revelation is inferior to the supernatural revelation and can only take us so far.

Every supernatural season has its own demands and rewards. Seasons prophesy telling us there is a spiritual harvest coming; a time of healing or a time of blessing. It is indeed a command of heaven that we prophesy over those who are internally fainting and those who are facing intense difficulties. They are to be reminded that the heat of

---

[290] *Luke 19:44 (LEB) — 44 And they will raze you to the ground, you and your children within you, and will not leave a stone upon a stone within you, because you did not recognize the time of your visitation."; Galatians 4:8–12 (LEB) — 8 But at that time when you did not know God, you were enslaved to the things which by nature are not gods. 9 But now, because you have come to know God, or rather have come to be known by God, how can you turn back again to the weak and miserable elemental spirits? Do you want to be enslaved to them all over again? 10 You carefully observe days and months and seasons and years. 11 I am afraid for you, lest perhaps I have laboured for you in vain! 12 I ask you, brothers, become like me, because I also have become like you. You have done me no wrong!; Galatians 4:8–12 (LEB) — 8 But at that time when you did not know God, you were enslaved to the things which by nature are not gods. 9 But now, because you have come to know God, or rather have come to be known by God, how can you turn back again to the weak and miserable elemental spirits? Do you want to be enslaved to them all over again? 10 You carefully observe days and months and seasons and years. 11 I am afraid for you, lest perhaps I have laboured for you in vain! 12 I ask you, brothers, become like me, because I also have become like you. You have done me no wrong!*

the battle will not overcome them.[291] It is important to understand that these prophetically determined words of scripture may speak more to the heart of the hearer, than the faith of the speaker. Regardless of whoever quotes them, God has already spoken them out as creative words.

The underlining faith of the prophet helps, but as in all true prophecy, the intended audience is the important person in the picture. Speaking for example, of those who have given up worldly possessions for the sake of the kingdom, the prophetic encouragement to such is that they will not fail in this life, to receive a commensurate reward.[292]

We are to watch out for these prophetically determined opportunities; like the one that existed for those who were sick to climb into the pool at Bethesda and to be healed once the angel had stirred the waters.[293]

---

[291] Isaiah 43:1–2 (LEB) — 1 But now thus says Yahweh, he who created you, Jacob, and he who formed you, Israel: "You must not fear, for I have redeemed you. I have called you by your name; you are mine. 2 When you pass through the waters, I will be with you, and through the rivers, they shall not flow over you. When you walk through fire, you shall not be burned, and the flame shall not scorch you.

[292] Mark 10:29–30 (LEB) — 29 Jesus said, "Truly I say to you, there is no one who has left house or brothers or sisters or mother or father or children or fields on account of me and on account of the gospel 30 who will not receive a hundred times as much now in this time—houses and brothers and sisters and mothers and children and fields, together with persecutions—and in the age to come, eternal life.

[293] John 5:3–5 (NKJV) — 3 In these lay a great multitude of sick people, blind, lame, paralyzed, waiting for the moving of the water. 4 For an angel went down at a certain time into the pool and stirred up the water; then whoever stepped in first, after the stirring of the water, was made well of whatever disease he had. 5 Now a certain man was there who had an infirmity thirty-eight years.

So, we understand there are some seasons which carry predetermined prophesied outcomes.[294] One might prophesy to an individual who has gone through a season of humility, to actively embrace the season because at the end of that season will come a time when God will exalt the individual in due course.[295] Or we might encourage an individual living a lifestyle less than honouring to the heavenly Father, to repent; that they may once more experience renewal and restoration.[296]

Whilst some eschatology seasons are closed to us[297] others are not, for example, we know that we are currently in the time of the Gentiles, a season that will see Jerusalem trampled on by the Gentiles until the time of the Gentiles are fulfilled,[298] a season when the word of God will not be honoured.[299]

Consequentially we should not be discouraged, it was prophesied. The ability of God to order time, space or indeed the life of every

---

[294] *Ecclesiastes 9:10 (LEB) — 10 Whatever your hand finds to do—do it with all your might; for in Sheol—where you are going—no one works, plans, knows, or thinks about anything.*

[295] *1 Peter 5:6 (LEB) — 6 Humble yourselves therefore under the mighty hand of God, so that he may exalt you at the right time,*

[296] *Acts 3:19 (LEB) — 19 Therefore repent and turn back, so that your sins may be blotted out,*

[297] *Acts 1:7 (LEB) — 7 But he said to them, "It is not for you to know the times or seasons that the Father has set by his own authority.*

[298] *Luke 21:24 (LEB) — 24 and they will fall by the edge of the sword, and will be led captive into all the nations, and Jerusalem will be trampled down by the Gentiles until the times of the Gentiles are fulfilled.*

[299] *2 Timothy 4:3 (LEB) — 3 For there will be a time when they will not put up with sound teaching, but in accordance with their own desires, they will accumulate for themselves teachers, because they have an insatiable curiosity,*

individual,[300] is not ultimately frustrated by the disobedience of man or the oppression of demons.[301] God has got his hands firmly on the rudder of time. The prophetic voice speaks into the heart of man, encouraging them to believe that they have been redeemed[302] and

---

[300] *Acts 17:26 (LEB) — 26 And he made from one man every nation of humanity to live on all the face of the earth, determining their fixed times and the fixed boundaries of their habitation,. (c/f) The Word is predetermined (proorizo)* <u>which means to mark out ahead of time</u>

[301] *Ephesians 6:10–12 (LEB) — 10 Finally, become strong in the Lord and in the might of his strength. 11 Put on the full armour of God, so that you may be able to stand against the stratagems of the devil, 12 because our struggle is not against blood and flesh, but against the rulers, against the authorities, against the world rulers of this darkness, against the spiritual forces of wickedness in the heavenly places.*

[302]   *We can offer liberty for the captive*

   Break the chains of oppression

   Provide for the dispossessed

   Reposes desolate places and in them proclaim Christ

   Sight for the blind

   Hope for the scourged

   Food for the hungry

   Rest for the weary

   Health for the sick

   Cast out demons

   Strengthen the feeble knees

   Break down strongholds

   And repair the broken down walls

   We can move mount

are being transformed into the likeness of Christ.[303] We look beyond what we can see to what he has said; knowing that he works everything out to the conformity of his will.[304] We have been given the right to minister this certainty, so we will be given the opportunity to prophesy it into people's lives.

Knowledge is power; and the brightest in society dedicate their minds to acquiring knowledge, whether it is those who work for MI5 or on the stock exchange, accountants or bankers, doctors or lawyers. For us, the scripture and knowledge of what our Father in heaven has conferred as the rights and privileges of his children, are key to the exercise of those rights.

When Moses faced the Red Sea, the prophetic wind gave him the right and authority to defy the laws of nature; he had the right to part the waters and so he did. When Peter stepped out the boat at the call of the master, he had the right to walk on water. When Moses encountered the burning bush, it was a supernatural event unlike anything he had ever witnessed before; he was alone, yet terrified as he drew near. To see God move and then to hesitate, is something many of us do.

The fact is, many believers on Sundays stand in the place where miracles happen but are not personally transformed because they do not personally draw close. They are in fact spectators; and as

---

[303] *Romans 8:29–30 (LEB) — 29 because those whom he foreknew, he also predestined to be conformed to the image of his Son, so that he should be the firstborn among many brothers. 30 And those whom he predestined, these he also called, and those whom he called, these he also justified, and those whom he justified, these he also glorified.*

[304] *Ephesians 1:11 (LEB) — 11 in whom also we were chosen, having been predestined according to the purpose of the One who works all things according to the counsel of his will,*

spectators, sin capitalises, taking opportunity away[305] because we choose our own path.[306]

When Paul had a vision of the man of Macedonia standing and begging,[307] Paul immediately responded. The simplicity of the response is contrasted by the challenge of the journey. This transition from the familiar to the challenging is for some, a bridge too far. Yet we were made for adventure, created to be missional.

When Moses accepted a call to lead God's people through the desert and untold challenges to a land filled with giants, Moses did not waver; he responded with faith. Faith calls for an investment of trust over reason, of holding on to the promises of God despite common sense[308]. As Christ was approaching his final days in Jerusalem he

---

[305] *Romans 7:7–9 (LEB) — 7 What then shall we say? Is the law sin? May it never be! But I would not have known sin except through the law, for I would not have known covetousness if the law had not said, "Do not covet." 8 But sin, seizing an opportunity through the commandment, produced in me all kinds of covetousness. For apart from the law, sin is dead. 9 And I was alive once, apart from the law, but when the commandment came, sin sprang to life*

[306] *Mat 16:21-23*

[307] *Acts 16:9–12 (LEB) — 9 And a vision appeared to Paul during the night: a certain Macedonian man was standing there and imploring him and saying, "Come over to Macedonia and help us!" 10 And when he had seen the vision, we wanted at once to go away to Macedonia, concluding that God had called us to proclaim the good news to them. 11 So putting out to sea from Troas, we sailed a straight course to Samothrace, and on the following day to Neapolis, 12 and from there to Philippi, which is a leading city of that district of Macedonia, a Roman colony. And we were staying in this city for some days.*

[308] *Hebrews 11:13–16 (LEB) — 13 These all died in faith without receiving the promises, but seeing them from a distance and welcoming them, and admitting that they were strangers and temporary residents on the earth. 14 For those who say such things make clear that they are seeking a homeland. 15 And if they remember that land from which they went out, they would have had opportunity to return. 16 But now they aspire to a better land, that is, a heavenly one. Therefore God is not ashamed of them, to be called their God, for he has prepared for them a city.*

knew that his appointed destiny was approaching[309], a destiny his mother had not missed and one that others had been aware of. The apostle Paul confirms that, just like Christ, there is an appointed, prepared destiny for us all,[310] just as there was for John the Baptist and just as Joseph realised when he became second to Pharaoh. In the end, God's prophetic mandate is influencing all our circumstances, and there is a cosmic plan.[311]

Once you have stood before your own personal burning bush, you will not be able to live without a deep sense of call burning in your heart[312], and hopefully you will take the opportunity afforded by heaven.

We are encouraged to be opportunists, to be standing on our toes ready to do good and bring God's word. We are not to let the darkness of the days terrorise, but through prophetic discharge, bring hope to every heart.

---

[309] *Mat 26:18 He replied, "Go into the city to a certain man and tell him, 'The Teacher says: My appointed time (kairos) near. I am going to celebrate the Passover with my disciples at your house.'" (NIV) (c/f) Luke 2:34 (LEB) — 34 And Simeon blessed them and said to his mother Mary, "Behold, this child is appointed for the fall and rise of many in Israel, and for a sign that is opposed—*

[310] *Ephesians 2:8–10 (LEB) — 8 For by grace you are saved through faith, and this is not from yourselves, it is the gift of God; 9 it is not from works, so that no one can boast. 10 For we are his creation, created in Christ Jesus for good works, which God prepared beforehand, so that we may walk in them.*

[311] *Romans 9:9–13 (LEB) — 9 For the statement of the promise is this: "At this time I will return and Sarah will have a son." 10 And not only this, but also when Rebecca conceived children by one man, Isaac our father—11 for although they had not yet been born, or done anything good or evil, in order that the purpose of God according to election might remain, 12 not by works but by the one who calls—it was said to her, "The older will serve the younger," 13 just as it is written, "Jacob I loved, but Esau I hated."*

[312] *Acts 26:16 (LEB) — 16 But get up and stand on your feet, because for this reason I have appeared to you, to appoint you a servant and witness both to the things in which you saw me and to the things in which I will appear to you, (c/f) 1 Corinthians 9:15-27*

The Father's Voice

Prophecy Demands Intimacy with God

When the human heart humbles itself and chooses to obey the prophetic call to repentance, man in Christ repossesses his original holiness.[313] He is able to stand in the divine presence just as the prophets of old, but this time not simply as messengers, but as sons and daughters.

Holiness, which means being set apart for God, is not arrived at as a result of institutional religion. It is not the result of works but has come about because of a prophetic promise of God, who showed his resolve to make us holy. His intent is seen in his steadfast commitment to generations of Abraham's descendants, binding himself to them in order to achieve his objective.[314]

---

[313] *Ephesians 4:23–24 (LEB) — 23 be renewed in the spirit of your mind, 24 and put on the new man (in accordance with God), who is created in righteousness and holiness from the truth. (C/f) Colossians 3:10 10 and have put on the new self, which is being renewed in knowledge in the image of its Creator. (NIV)*

[314] *Genesis 17:7 (LEB) — 7 And I will establish my covenant between me and you, and between your offspring after you, throughout their generations as an everlasting covenant to be as God for you and to your offspring after you.*

God's original intent was that Israel herself was to be a holy nation, a nation of priests;[315] indicating that the whole nation was meant to have a sense of being set apart and chosen for God's purposes. Those who currently live a holy life touch on the conscience of those who don't; it makes them aware of a future that is awaited by all. Thus, it is an aid to present morality.[316]

The heavenly court in which the prophet stands proves that there is no point serving any other God; for no other has revealed the distant future. In a search of all other religious text, it becomes clear that no other god knows the future.[317]

Only God has told of things long before they happen.[318] In case his grasp of time is lost on a present generation, he shows he is not just the God who can see the distant future, but that he can predict

---

[315] *Exodus 19:5–6 (LEB) — 5 And now if you will carefully listen to my voice and keep my covenant, you will be a treasured possession for me out of all the peoples, for all the earth is mine, 6 but you, you will belong to me as a kingdom of priests and a holy nation.' These are the words that you will speak to the Israelites."*

[316] *2 Peter 3:11 (NIV) — 11 Since everything will be destroyed in this way, what kind of people ought you to be? You ought to live holy and godly lives*

[317] *Isaiah 41:25-27 "I have stirred up one from the north, and he comes--one from the rising sun who calls on my name. He treads on rulers as if they were mortar, as if he were a potter treading the clay. 26 Who told of this from the beginning, so we could know, or beforehand, so we could say, `He was right'? No one told of this, no one foretold it, no one heard any words from you. 27 I was the first to tell Zion, `Look, here they are!' I gave to Jerusalem a messenger of good tidings. (NIV)*

[318] *Isaiah 48:5 Therefore I told you these things long ago; before they happened I announced them to you so that you could not say, `My idols did them; my wooden image and metal god ordained them.' (NIV)*

incredible miracles moments before they happened. By this, people discover that God is amongst them.[319]

Through knowledge of the prophetic, faith grows. Joseph knew long before it happened that God's prophetic intention was to deliver his people from Egypt, even before their need for deliverance became clear, and long before their circumstances changed for the worse.[320]

In declaring his intent, God highlights Pharaoh's inability to prevent the departure of the Hebrew slave people from Pharaoh's land. Even now as we recount the story, it encourages our faith.[321] Similarly, David knew that the people of God would be strengthened in their

---

[319] *Joshua 3:10-13 This is how you will know that the living God is among you and that he will certainly drive out before you the Canaanites, Hittites, Hivites, Perizzites, Girgashites, Amorites and Jebusites. 11 See, the ark of the covenant of the Lord of all the earth will go into the Jordan ahead of you. 12 Now then, choose twelve men from the tribes of Israel, one from each tribe. 13 And as soon as the priests who carry the ark of the LORD-the Lord of all the earth-set foot in the Jordan, its waters flowing downstream will be cut off and stand up in a heap." (C/f) Joshua 4:14 That day the LORD exalted Joshua in the sight of all Israel; and they revered him all the days of his life, just as they had revered Moses. (C/f) Joshua 3:7 And the LORD said to Joshua, "Today I will begin to exalt you in the eyes of all Israel, so they may know that I am with you as I was with Moses. (NIV)*

[320] *Genesis 50:24–25 (NKJV) — 24 And Joseph said to his brethren, "I am dying; but God will surely visit you, and bring you out of this land to the land of which He swore to Abraham, to Isaac, and to Jacob." 25 Then Joseph took an oath from the children of Israel, saying, "God will surely visit you, and you shall carry up my bones from here."*

Hebrews 11:22 (NKJV) — 22 By faith Joseph, when he was dying, made mention of the departure of the children of Israel, and gave instructions concerning his bones.

[321] *John 14:29 (NKJV) — 29 "And now I have told you before it comes, that when it does come to pass, you may believe.*

faith when they saw Goliath fall, and so he prophesied it to those gathered.[322]

His personal knowledge of God's ability to keep covenantal promises was gained in the face of danger while looking after his father's sheep. This previous experience was the confidence behind David's prophetic pronouncement before he faced Goliath, and what underpinned his faith.[323] Every promise of God is a prophecy.

The Lord's forecast of blessing and safe conduct to Canaan was twice claimed in prayer by another hero of faith, Jacob. When Jacob was about to meet his brother Esau, he was afraid about how he would be received because this was the brother he had cheated out of the inheritance of the firstborn. He needed reassurance and comforted himself by reminding God of his promises. Reminding God about

---

[322] *1 Samuel 17:46–47 (NKJV) — 46 This day the LORD will deliver you into my hand, and I will strike you and take your head from you. And this day I will give the carcasses of the camp of the Philistines to the birds of the air and the wild beasts of the earth, that all the earth may know that there is a God in Israel. 47 Then all this assembly shall know that the LORD does not save with sword and spear; for the battle is the LORD's, and He will give you into our hands."*

[323] *1 Samuel 17:37 (NIV) The LORD who delivered me from the paw of the lion and the paw of the bear will deliver me from the hand of this Philistine." Saul said to David, "Go, and the LORD be with you."*

those prophecies was in effect for Jacob, an aid to faith,[324] channelling his emotions back to a place of peace, where he could trust and worship.[325]

Through repetition and declaration, as seen in Jacobs's regurgitation of God's promises to him, prophecy becomes an aid to worship; an anchor for the soul and an enabler of devotion and courage in the journey of life. A few people truly understand the power of declaration,[326] though many should understand the benefits of repetition.

---

[324] *Genesis 32:9–12 (NKJV) — 9 Then Jacob said, "O God of my father Abraham and God of my father Isaac, the LORD who said to me, 'Return to your country and to your family, and I will deal well with you': 10 I am not worthy of the least of all the mercies and of all the truth which You have shown Your servant; for I crossed over this Jordan with my staff, and now I have become two companies. 11 Deliver me, I pray, from the hand of my brother, from the hand of Esau; for I fear him, lest he come and attack me and the mother with the children. 12 For You said, 'I will surely treat you well, and make your descendants as the sand of the sea, which cannot be numbered for multitude.' "; Genesis 28:15–21 (NKJV) — 15 Behold, I am with you and will keep you wherever you go, and will bring you back to this land; for I will not leave you until I have done what I have spoken to you." 16 Then Jacob awoke from his sleep and said, "Surely the LORD is in this place, and I did not know it." 17 And he was afraid and said, "How awesome is this place! This is none other than the house of God, and this is the gate of heaven!" 18 Then Jacob rose early in the morning, and took the stone that he had put at his head, set it up as a pillar, and poured oil on top of it. 19 And he called the name of that place Bethel; but the name of that city had been Luz previously. 20 Then Jacob made a vow, saying, "If God will be with me, and keep me in this way that I am going, and give me bread to eat and clothing to put on, 21 so that I come back to my father's house in peace, then the LORD shall be my God.*

[325] *Genesis 35:1-5 Then God said to Jacob, "Go up to Bethel and settle there, and build an altar there to God, who appeared to you when you were fleeing from your brother Esau." 2 So Jacob said to his household and to all who were with him, "Get rid of the foreign gods you have with you, and purify yourselves and change your clothes. 3 Then come, let us go up to Bethel, where I will build an altar to God, who answered me in the day of my distress and who has been with me wherever I have gone." 4 So they gave Jacob all the foreign gods they had and the rings in their ears, and Jacob buried them under the oak at Shechem. 5 Then they set out, and the terror of God fell upon the towns all around them so that no one pursued them. NIV*

[326] <u>*The power of declaration*</u> *; Is seen in God creative acts Gen 1; Is seen in David's declaration to Goliath*

The Sustaining Voice

This voice from heaven, literally seen vibrating through the shimmering of created stars, sustains heaven. The voice that comes down to us from heaven brings light, hope and direction; it feeds the spirit. Just as bread feeds the body, the words of God are mysteriously connected, so as to be 'The Bread of Heaven' who became[327] flesh;[328] he is that which inexplicably proceeds from the Father, the very Word of God.

Just as the people of God ate manna, the food of angels in the desert, God by his spoken word feeds us.[329] Prophetic metaphors and analogies take us into the realm of spiritually illuminating brilliance, requiring the gentle explanation of the Father to tease out strands of light for us and give us an explanation.

When Jesus sat beside the woman at the well, he took time to explain to her the implications of asking for living water; he opened her spiritual eyes. The voice from heaven takes on different forms and must be received in the form from which it is coming. His disciples had to recognise that this prophetic voice from heaven comes in the metaphoric form of bread, which must become our meat. When Jesus used this metaphor, it implied a literal partaking of his flesh and

---

[327] I am the light of the world John 8:12 ; I am the gate john 10:7; I am the good shepherd john 10:17 ; I am the resurrection and the life john 11:25 ; I am the way the truth and the life john 14L6 ; I am the true vine john 15:1

[328] John 6:33 (NIV)] For the bread of God is he who comes down from heaven and gives life to the world."

[329] John 6:29-32 (NIV) Jesus answered, "The work of God is this: to believe in the one he has sent." [30] So they asked him, "What miraculous sign then will you give that we may see it and believe you? What will you do? [31] Our forefathers ate the manna in the desert; as it is written: 'He gave them bread from heaven to eat.'"[32] Jesus said to them, "I tell you the truth, it is not Moses who has given you the bread from heaven, but it is my Father who gives you the true bread from heaven.

blood; a thought that made many disciples who had been following Christ take offence and leave him.[330] But Christ, as we know, was speaking of spiritual matters not literal.

The prophetic necessity[331] to eat is not withdrawn in the face of a lack of understanding. Jesus points out that their inability to understand comes out of a lack of relationship. Unless the Father is heard and understood, no one can receive the Christ or his words.[332]

Longing for Home

It was always God's intention that we should live as a son or daughter; meaning living a lifestyle which is manifestly led by his Spirit, which is one of his key objectives.

> *Romans 8:15 (NIV) For you did not receive a spirit that makes you a slave again to fear, but you received the Spirit of sonship. And by him, we cry, "Abba, Father."*

God is our Father and heaven is his home. Heaven is that part of eternity that humanity instinctively longs to see. For almost every human intuition of heaven, there is the antithesis; a place no one wants to mention, everyone thinks of, and few elect to go. Despite the hazy notions about heaven and hell, we all long for an eternal home and desire to know our eternal Father. In lucid moments everyone ponders on what eternity will mean for them, often just a moment's thought, sometimes lingering. We are initially, to all intents

---

[330] John 6:60

[331] Matthew 10:32-33 (NIV) "Whoever acknowledges me before men, I will also acknowledge him before my Father in heaven. [33] But whoever disowns me before men, I will disown him before my Father in heaven.

[332] John 6:65 (NIV) [65] He went on to say, "This is why I told you that no one can come to me unless the Father has enabled him."

and purposes, metaphorically lost,[333] not able in any spiritual sense to find our way home.

Then heaven surprises us and God illuminates; he speaks to us out of the blue; we hear his prophetic voice, recognising the strangely familiar tones. For Jacob, the act of going to sleep was such a moment. Jacob put his head down to retire for the night and encountered God where he slept. Having had a dream in which he saw angels ascending and descending from heaven, he made the declaration *"this is none other than the house of God, the gates of heaven"*.[334]

The impact of such occasions is definitive; spiritual eyes become opened to supernatural realities. For every Christian there has already been one such illumination of God; it is called conversion, being born again, or coming to faith; but there can be so many more such experiences of God.

The Eternal and the Internal Longing of a Son

I have a four-year-old son who is madly in love with his mum. She is the only one in our home who gets lingering cuddles, and I get two-second hugs, she is his world. His two older brothers and I have to be content with whatever crumbs of affection he has left to grant us after he has lavished reservoirs of love on his mother. Like him, we all have an insatiable longing for our heavenly Father. Our internal compass (thoughts, emotions and spirit) and external compass (what we see, hear and feel), point us towards the supernatural because he has made us eternal beings. So, when we gaze at the stars, we see the

---

[333] *The consequences of being metaphorically lost ; We need to be found Mat 18:11*

[334] *Genesis 28:12-17*

hand of a designer and watch them with an awe that resonates with the sense of destiny embedded in our hearts.

Instinctively we know this life will not be the final chapter, we will rise again. Hence Christians are usually confident of resurrection. Whether Christian or not, humanity instinctively knows that the just and unjust alike are ever-living persons. This is why over 99% of the world's population believe in an afterlife of some kind. In the trail of a spiritual awakening, the spiritually aware live different lifestyles to the general populace. Although there is much evil in the world, most live a life motivated by love. The transient nature of this world been etched on the soul. Even unbelievers recognise and speak of "heaven" as the place where believers go at the point of death and "hell" as the place where unbelievers go. It is this longing for eternity that draws people into a variety of spiritual experiences, and demonic forces use this to entice people into false religions.

Eventually, the searching heart finds that heaven is much more than just a watering hole in the sky; more than the great retirement home in glory; more than a blissful eternal worship service. We may legally be sons and daughters, but it is only through the function of the spirit in our lives that we live as sons and daughters on earth, making the influence of the Father itself a present reality. God steadily reveals his glory to us, just as he did on the mount of transfiguration and speaks to that internal longing.

If every individual is meant to have relational integrity with our heavenly Father, how much more then should those who spiritually lead us have? They ought to be in tune with spiritual realities, rather than blind to them. Jesus had some choice words to say to the teachers of the law and the Pharisees, who at times did not understand even the simplest of prophetic typology, like the weight they should give to swearing by the altar, as opposed to the weight they should give to swearing by the gift on the altar.[335] Their personal lack of relational integrity and therefore spiritual blindness, had the effect of shutting up heaven to those who followed them.[336]

A Relationship that Produces Security

The Ruach, or voice of God, resonates through time to bring us into that relationship with a loving and divine Father. John the Baptist's first lesson about the Christ was on the nature of Christ's relationship with heaven, "this is my beloved son", a son-ship based on love. Christ already knew his place and purpose in relationship to heaven and in that sense was secure. It is interesting to note that John the Baptist also carried a sense of security, knowing who he was in God's purposes. He was happy to decrease in stature so that Christ might increase in prominence. His sense of belonging was not so tied to his office that he could not let it go, demonstrating through his attitude the kingdom value of humility.

---

[335] *Matthew 23:16-24 (NIV)]* "Woe to you, blind guides! You say, 'If anyone swears by the temple, it means nothing; but if anyone swears by the gold of the temple, he is bound by his oath.' [17] You blind fools! Which is greater: the gold, or the temple that makes the gold sacred? [18] You also say, 'If anyone swears by the altar, it means nothing; but if anyone swears by the gift on it, he is bound by his oath.' [19] You blind men! Which is greater: the gift, or the altar that makes the gift sacred? [20] Therefore, he who swears by the altar swears by it and by everything on it. [21] And he who swears by the temple swears by it and by the one who dwells in it. [22] And he who swears by heaven swears by God's throne and by the one who sits on it. [23] "Woe to you, teachers of the law and Pharisees, you hypocrites! You give a tenth of your spices—mint, dill and cummin. But you have neglected the more important matters of the law—justice, mercy and faithfulness. You should have practiced the latter, without neglecting the former. [24] You blind guides! You strain out a gnat but swallow a camel.*

[336] *Matthew 23:13 (NIV) "Woe to you, teachers of the law and Pharisees, you hypocrites! You shut the kingdom of heaven in men's faces. You yourselves do not enter, nor will you let those enter who are trying to.*

"Kingdom values are lived out of an understanding of identity."

When Christ begins to preach we see a clear succession from John the Baptist, and his message is exactly the same as John's message. Jesus began to call for repentance because heaven was near. In and through Jesus, heaven established a bridgehead on earth. His coming brought a permanent shift, a restoration of divine order in the human heart, and a permanent bridge between heaven and earth. In him, the divine and human is forever joined, imposing divine purpose for humanity and forever establishing a breach between the spiritual and material, heaven and earth, God and man. While the garden represents the greatest breakdown of relationship in history, it also reveals the promise of the greatest reconciliation of broken relationship, for it was in the Garden of Eden that this coming of Christ was prophesied.

APPENDIX A

REFLECTING ON FIVE OF MANY ACCURATE PROPHECIES IN THE BIBLE

The prophecy that Ben Haddad's forces were to slay Ahab and repel Israel at Ramoh-Gilead.

1. On the first attack the prophet had originally prophesied that Ben Haddad's army was going to be delivered to Ahab which subsequently took place, 1 Kings 20:13-21

2. 1 Kings 20:22–27

3. But on the second attack, Ben Haddad was to return with enough force to fill the country in an attempt to take Israel.

4. The prophet again prophesied that Ahab would be delivered a second time into the hands of Israel, 1 Kings 20:28-30

5. But Ahab did not kill Ben Haddad resulting in God's disapproval, 1 Kings 20:31-37

6. The prophet decreed that for sparing Ben Haddad's life Ahab would lose his, 1 Kings 20:42-43

7. Not believing the word he later had Micah imprisoned but he was never to return from Ramoth Gilead where the Lord had him put to death, this was fulfilled in 857, 1 Kings 22:19-29

The Prophecy of Agabus concerning a famine which he predicted would affect the Roman world.

1. Acts 11:28 (NKJV) — 28 Then one of them, named Agabus, stood up and showed by the Spirit that there was going to be a great famine throughout all the world, which also happened in the days of Claudius Caesar. (This happened during the reign of Claudius 41-54 ad.)

2. As a result, the church was prepared and able to send relief missions. Acts 11:30 This they did, sending their gift to the elders by Barnabas and Saul. (C/f) Acts 12:25 When Barnabas and Saul had finished their mission, they returned from Jerusalem, taking with them John, also called Mark.

Jeremiah makes the short-term prophecy one year in advance as a sign of fulfilment of an event to take place in the future

1. Hophra was dethroned and executed by Amasis in 569.

2. Jeremiah 44:29-30 "`This will be the sign to you that I will punish you in this place,' declares the LORD, `so that you will know that my threats of harm against you will surely stand.' 30 This is what the LORD says: `I am going to hand Pharaoh Hophra king of Egypt over to his enemies who seek his life, just as I handed Zedekiah king of Judah over to Nebuchadnezzar king of Babylon, the enemy who was seeking his life.'"

Jeroboams alter, and the man of God validated long-range prophecy about Josiah coming 308 years later

1. 1 Kings 13:1-22

2. FULFILMENT 2 Kings 23:15-17

Prophecies around the death of Christ

1. Isaiah 53:9-10

2. Daniel 9:26

3. Zechariah 11:12

Endnotes

[i] **GROWTH OF CHURCH IN NATIONS**
Ad 100 1st [i] By the end of the first century the world population was around 180 million people with around 1 million Christian 6%
312 CE, when emperor Constantine, the leader of the Roman Empire, converted to Christianity.
- In 1430 one in 99 of the world's population were Christians. [i]
- In 1790 one in 49
- In 1940 one in 32
- In 1970 one in 19
- In 1980 one in 16
- In 1983 one in 13
- In 1986 one in 11
- In 1994 one in 10
- Now one in three
- In the period 1934-1994, the number of Christians in the world increased by 1300 percent (from 40 million to 540 million in the last 60 years), while the world's population grew only 400 percent.

(The Lausanne Statistics Task Force, cited in Grant R. Jeffrey *Final Warning*, Harvest House publishers, Eugene, Oregon, 1996, pages. 251-254)

Printed in Poland
by Amazon Fulfillment
Poland Sp. z o.o., Wrocław